TITLE:

VISIBLE MUSIC

CD JACKET GRAPHIC

AUTHOR:

VISIBLE MUSIC

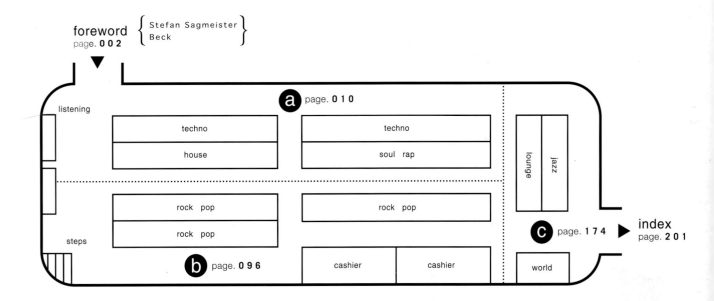
COPYRIGHT© 2000 BY P·I·E BOOKS

EDITORIAL NOTES

CREDIT FORMAT: Title Artist Label Released Year Country (Label) CD Number
CREATIVE STAFF: CD: Creative Director AD: Art Director D: Designer P: Photographer
　　　　　　　　　 I: Illustrator CW: Copy Writer DF: Design Firm

ＣＤのレーベル名は国によってそれぞれ異なりますが、本書では弊社が掲載の許可をいただいたレーベル名を記載させていただきました。また、国名は、そのレーベルの所在する国です。

The names of CD companies often vary by country. Names used in this book are those of the companies from which publication permission was obtained, and the country indicated is that of said company.

掲載した作品の中には編集作業の間にレーベルの移動やレコード会社が変わったものもあります。
The record companies and labels of several featured CDs changed during the editing this book.

デザインクレジットは、掲載の許可をいただく際にその要望があったもののみ記載させていただきました。
The record companies and labels of several featured CDs changed during the editing this book.

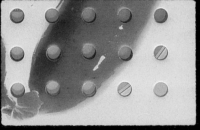

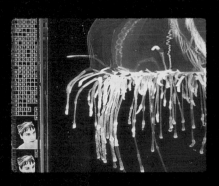

Stefan
Sagmeister
ステファン・サグマイスター

Stefan Sagmeister, a native of Austria, received his MFA in graphic design from the University of Applied Arts in Vienna and, as a Fulbright Scholar, a master's degree from Pratt Institute in New York.

He formed the New York based Sagmeister Inc. in 1993 and has since designed graphics and packaging for the Rolling Stones, David Byrne, Lou Reed, Aerosmith and Pat Metheny. His work has been nominated four times for the Grammies and has won most international design awards.

He lives in New York and loves Anni.

オーストリア生まれ。ウィーンのユニバーシティ・オブ・アプライド・アーツでグラフィックデザインの修士号MFAを取得。またフルブライト奨学生としてニューヨークのプラット・インスティテュートで修士を取得している。

1993年にニューヨークをベースにサグマイスター社を設立、以来、ローリングストーンズ、デヴィッド・バーン、ルー・リード、エアロスミス、パット・メセニーなどのグラフィックスやパッケージングを手がけている。作品はこれまで4回グラミー賞にノミネートされており、多くの国際デザイン賞を受賞している。

ニューヨーク在住、Anniを愛している。

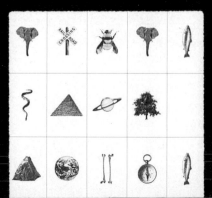

I love designing CD covers. I love spending serious time designing something that is going to be so tiny. I love to meet up with my musical heroes (much more fun than sitting in meetings with marketing managers) and I love that I never have to schlepp my portfolio anywhere around the world: I can just go to the next record store and buy it.

What I like most about it though is to come up with ideas simply by listening to music. We normally meet with the band 3-4 months before we deliver artwork, listen to rough cuts from the studio and get their view of the album. At this point I normally avoid talking about the cover and concentrate on lyrics/album title/song titles instead. We then play the music for a couple of weeks without even starting the design.

In the mid-eighties, when compact discs first made a serious impact on the record industry, designers and art directors didn't stop to complain about the horrible consequences of the switch from the beloved 12-inch album to the tiny CD package. Apart from the general whining about the minuscule size, there was tons of moaning about the material: What was once stiff cardboard, specified in different finishes, embossed and die-cut, will now be flimsy paper stuffed into a plastic box. And they were right: Record companies reduced existing album art work down, slapped some larger type on it and sold the whole thing as CD packaging. Not surprisingly, the impact of the original was lost.

All this has changed: Designers got familiar with the new format and its capabilities, projects are started with the jewel box in mind and the results are astonishing: There are a number of CD's on the market that rival or top the best 12-inch album covers. Designers like Peter Saville, Mark Farrow, Vaughan Oliver, Me Company, Tomato do some of their best work on CD covers.

Having said that, it is a real challenge for a designer to come up with a striking package while staying within the confinements of that ugly plastic jewel box. Those specialty CD covers made out of metal or wood or whatnot, published for promotional purposes and delivered to radio stations and music magazines, with leftovers sold at horrendous prices

as collectors items, seem like a cop-out: Any idiot can come up with something eye-catching with an unlimited production budget.

From a record company's point of view, a CD cover has to fulfill two requirements: First it has to visually interpret the music. Secondly, it should entice a customer to pick it up while browsing in a record store. There is quite some discussion within the industry if a great cover actually sells more CD's. Some record company executives who think the cover doesn't really have an impact on sales often mention Michael Jackson's Thriller, which sold millions utilizing a decidedly run-of-the mill cover. However, our own experience suggests otherwise: The cover we designed for H. P. Zinker in 1993 was issued with an altered, weaker design for its cassette release. The CD outsold the cassette 2 to 1, quite a difference considering the then industry standard in this segment of 50% CDs to 50% cassettes.

The inside graphics of the booklet and the actual CD serve an entirely different purpose: Since they are concealed during the buying process, they're almost like a 'Thank You' from the artist. Apart from displaying lyrics and liner notes, they should make the consumer feel good about the band. A typical CD cover holds much more information than its vinyl counterpart. While album covers were almost like posters, CD covers are closer related to book design. 20-page booklets, transparent trays with concealed graphics underneath the CD, and elaborate printing are seen on many general releases.

In a couple of years they will seem as outdated as vinyl now: MP3 is here to stay and the combined computer/TV/music center in every household a real possibility. Widespread downloading of music seems likely, demanding new forms of downloadable packaging with completely new possibilities and challenges.

At the end, the old adage will still be true: The best music packaging is only as good as the music it packages. If the contents are bullshit, so is the packaging.

私はＣＤジャケットをデザインするのが好きだ。これほど小さなものに、かなりの時間をかけてデザインするのが好きなのである。自分の音楽のヒーローに出会うことも好きである（マーケティング担当者との打ち合わせで座っているよりずっと楽しい）。そして、世界じゅうにポートフォリオを持ち運ぶ必要がないのもいい。近所のレコード屋へ行って、買えばよいのだから。

しかし、私が最も好きなのは、アイデアを練るために単に音楽を聞けばよいことである。通常、アートワークを納品する3〜4ヶ月前にはバンドのメンバーと会い、スタジオでのラフな音を聞いてアルバムに対する彼らの考えを把握する。この時点では、私はいつもカバーに関して話すのは避け、詞やアルバムのタイトル、ソングタイトルなどに集中するようにしている。その後2〜3週間は、デザイン作業に入ることなく、その音楽を聞き続けるのである。

80年代半ば、ＣＤが最初にレコード業界に大きなインパクトを与えはじめた頃、デザイナーやアートディレクターは、愛すべき12インチのＬＰから小さなＣＤパッケージに移行するという残酷な結果に不平を言ってやまなかった。その極めて小さいというサイズ一般に対する不満を別としても、素材についても山のような不平が聞かれた。エンボスやダイカットなど様々な仕上げを指定できた固いボール紙が、いまやプラスチックのケースに納まったペラペラの紙である。そして彼らの不満は当たっていた。レコード会社は単に既存のアルバムのアートワークを縮小し、いくらか大きめのタイポをポンとくっつけ、すべてをＣＤパッケージとして売り出したのである。当然ながら、オリジナルの持っていたインパクトは失われてしまった。

しかし、これらすべてのことは変わった。今やデザイナーは新しいフォーマットとその可能性に慣れ、プロジェクトはプラスチックのケースを念頭においてスタートするようになり、結果は驚くべきものとなっている。市場には優れた12インチのアルバム・ジャケットに匹敵する、あるいはそれらに勝るほどのＣＤも登場している。ピーター・サヴィル、マーク・ファロウ、ヴォーン・オリバー、ミー・カンパニー、トマトなどは、非常に優れたＣＤジャケット作品を残している。

しかし、醜いプラスチックケースという制限のなかで優れたパッケージを考え出すことは、デザイナーにとっては非常に難しい。プロモーション用にラジオ局や音楽雑誌などに配布され、残りはコレクターズアイテムとしてものすごい価格で売買されるような、メタルや木やその他でできた特別製のＣＤジャケットならたやすいものである。どんな素人でも、十分な予算さえあれば何かしら目を引くようなものを考えつくことはできるのだから。

レコード会社の視点から言えば、ＣＤジャケットは2つの要件を満たしていなければならない。まず最初に、視覚的に音楽を解説するものでなければならない。二番目に、レコード店で客が商品を眺めているときに手に取ってみたくなるようなものでなければならない。業界では、優れたＣＤジャケットは本当により売れるのかという論議がある。ジャケットはセールスには影響しないと主張するレコード会社の重役は、よくマイケル・ジャクソンの『スリラー』について言及する。ありふれた出来栄えと誰もが認めるようなジャケットを使用して何百万枚と売れた。しかし、我々は経験からそうではないことを知っている。1993年にＨ.Ｐ.Zinkerのために CDのジャケット・デザインを手がけたが、カセットのリリースにあたってデザインは変更され、弱いデザインとなった。この時、ＣＤの売れ行きがカセットに対して2対1となったが、この分野では業界の標準がＣＤ50％、カセット50％であるのを考えるとかなりの差である。

ブックレットの中ページのグラフィックスとＣＤ本体は全く異なった目的を持っている。これらは、買うという過程においては隠されているため、買った人へアーティストから『ありがとう』を伝える部分とも言える。詞とライナーノートを見せるという他にも、購入者がバンドに対して良い感覚を抱くようにしなければならない。一般的にＣＤジャケットは、ＬＰよりも多くの情報を持っている。アルバムのジャケットがポスター的なのに対し、ＣＤジャケットはブックデザインにより近い。20ページのブックレット、透明なトレーとＣＤの下に隠されたグラフィックス、華やかな印刷などは、多くのリリースでよく見られる手法である。

しかし、いまやＬＰがそうであるように、ＣＤも数年のうちに時代遅れになっていくようである。ＭＰ3が出現したことで、どの家庭にもコンピューター、テレビ、音楽を組み合わせた機器があるようになる。音楽をダウンロードすることが普及し、全く新しい可能性とチャレンジを備えたダウンロード可能なパッケージングという新しいフォームが要求されている。

最後に、古いことわざにある真実を述べたい。『パッケージングが非常に優れていれば、その中の音楽も同じくらい優れたものである。』音楽がひどければパッケージもまたしかり、である。

SET THE TWILIGHT REELING *LOU REED*

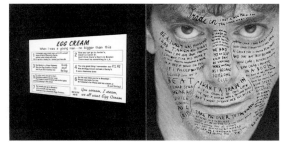

booklet

front

NINE LIVES *AEROSMITH*

booklet

front

BRIDGES TO BABYLON *ROLLING STONES*

inner with disk

front

Beck ベック

Beck Hansen was born and raised in Los Angeles.

1993 Single "Loser" (Bongload Custom Recordings)
Album "Golden Feelings" (Sonic Enemy)

1994 Album "A Western Harvest Field by Moonlight"
(Fingerpaint Records)
Album "Stereopathetic Soulmanure"
(Gusto Productions/Flipside Records)
Album "Mellow Gold" (Geffen/DGC Records)
Album "One Foot in the Grave" (K Records)

1996 Album "Odelay" (Geffen Records) won him two Grammys,
for the Best Alternative Performance and Best Male Vocal
Performance.

1998 Beck helped put together an art installation that paired his
own work with that of his late grandfather, Fluxus pioneer
Al Hansen. "Beck and Al Hansen: Playing With Matches"
made its debut at the Santa Monica Museum of Art.
It came to the Laforet Gallery, Tokyo Japan in 1999.

1998 Album "Mutations" (Geffen Records)
1999 Album "Midnite Vultures" (Geffen Records)

2000 Beck just won another Grammy award for
"Best Alternative Album" for "Mutations".

ロサンゼルス出身。

1993 シングル『Loser』(Bongload Custom Recordings)
アルバム『Golden Feelings』(Sonic Enemy)

1994 アルバム『A Western Harvest Field by Moonlight』
(Fingerpaint Records)
アルバム『Stereopathetic Soulmanure』
(Gusto Productions/Flipside Records)
アルバム『Mellow Gold』(Geffen/DGC Records)
アルバム『One Foot in the Grave』(K Records)

1996 アルバム『Odelay』(Geffen Records)
ベスト・オルタナティブ・パフォーマンスおよびベスト・メール・
ヴォーカル・パフォーマンスの2つのグラミー賞を受賞。

1998 フルクサスの開拓者である祖父アル・ハンセンとインスタレー
ション『Beck and Al Hansen: Playing With Matches』を共同
制作。サンタモニカ美術館で初の展覧会を行う。1999年、東京
のラフォーレ・ミュージアムで巡回展。

1998 アルバム『Mutations』(Geffen Records)
1999 アルバム『Midnite Vultures』(Geffen Records)
2000 『Mutations』でグラミー賞、ベスト・オルタナティブ・
アルバムを受賞

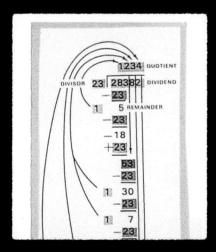

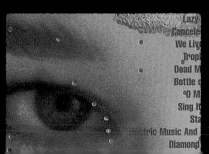

What does the artwork express?

With Odelay, the cover communicated honor and optimism. Inside, the imagery becomes more complex and chaotic. The collage of artwork by Ocampo, Al Hansen and myself served as a conscious visual reference for the music on the album. It was meant to be a physical map of the music, something to guide you through the songs. As a kid I would stare at a record I liked over and over, as if it could tell me something I didn't know about the songs or the musicians. I think the music video has taken away from this, somewhat. We get our important visual information about an artist from them now. But a certain mystery is possible with the silent imagery of an album.

With Tropicalia it was important to express a lightness and clarity. There is a predominance of white space, and the clarity of the keyboard; the notes of the scale laid out orderly. There is a sensual intelligence inherent in bossa nova music, so this was what needed to be communicated in the image. Also, the song is a bit retro, so the image was graphic in a late 60's science book way.

The photo on the Mutations cover is a snapshot of me backstage in Buffalo, New York, with a dry cleaning bag over me. We had done extensive photo shoots for the cover, but they didn't seem natural and didn't communicate the ease and spirit of the music. My girlfriend Leigh noticed this photo and said we should use it. It seemed like a throwaway, but we tried it (we cut out the background, which was a dressing room trailer) and it worked well.

How did you actually do the artwork?

The artwork is usually taken from photos, collages and drawings which are fed into the computer and assembled using various graphics programs. With Odelay, the cover was taken from a dog book, as simple as that. Some color correcting was involved, but that's it. The inside was more involved. I sat with the layout designer for several days creating the inside collage on a computer. We scanned in many images, then manipulated them, cut them up, and arranged them until we achieved a compositional whole. This involved much trial and error. Sometimes we erased an image to create a residual graphic outline of the image. I was doing drawings as we worked and then scanning them in and layering them over the collage. An additive process, much like the way we recorded it. I wanted it to communicate chaos and color, but be connected and flowing. With the Tropicalia single, we used a detail from a collage I did manually with scissors and glue.

How did you select the creator for the jacket design?

He was the staff designer at the record label. Initially, he was assigned to me. We worked on three albums together.

Who did the logo type?

I usually request books and books of type and search for one I like. Then I have the designer lay out a bunch of possibilities and I pick ones that match the image. There are always types that are trendy. I try to use ones that are out of date. The western type on Odelay provided a hokey contrast to the music. (I guess some of the music was hokey, too). With Mutations we created the type from scratch. I find this necessary now. All my new releases have original type.

What is the connection between the artwork and the music?

Creating an image to represent music you've poured your heart and soul into is difficult because it is so important. It colors our perception of the music so thoroughly. It whets our appetite for the sounds therein. The image represents a visual reference for the music that is permanent. When I think back to my favorite albums, the artwork is the first thing that flashes in my mind. The classic albums were an event, a cultural identifier. The new Stones record would speak as loud as their music. The Beatles with Revolver and Sgt. Pepper distilled their aesthetic sound and personality. The marriage of a sound and image is more accidental and instinctual than manufactured. I'm talking about a true image marriage. More often than not the planned cover has been scrapped in my case, and a seemingly random one used instead. Yet in time this image always seems to endure as the appropriate image for the music. In the case of Odelay, the cover was extremely overdue, and I had no ideas.

While flipping through a book on dogs I came upon the image of the Komondor leaping over the hurdle. The image struck me as humorous, yet aesthetically pleasing, with its primary colors of blue sky, red and white on the hurdle. It had a pleasing graphic quality that was simple and immediate. I also identified with this image because I too felt like I'd just leaped over a hurdle after spending a year creating this record.

I think the most important factor to consider in regard to the contemporary album cover is the size of a CD. The limitations of space imposed by this format have changed our approach tremendously. Only so much will read on such a small surface. On my album covers I try to limit one figure or object to a cover; two maximum. So, with this limitation we've had to simplify, be less ambitious.

Conversely, the inside artwork space has expanded, so now we have booklets (sequential images) and pullouts with 10 or 12 panels. I think we are still adjusting to this size format. Finding out what translates well with it. Re-thinking the approach is essential. Thinking with these limitations in mind is essential. Because the songs on my albums tend to create an aggregate whole, I tend to use the pullout insert so I can create a continuous stream of images that vary yet still connect.

アートワークは何を表現しているか。

『Odelay』のジャケットは、敬意と楽観を表している。中ページでは
イメージはより複雑で、混沌としている。オカンポ、アル・ハンセン
そして僕の3名によるコラージュ作品は、アルバムの曲の視覚的な
リファレンスとなるよう意識した。曲から曲への道案内になるような、
形而的な音楽地図となるよう意図した。子供の頃、好きなレコードの
ジャケットをくり返し見つめていたものだが、そうすることで、曲や
そのミュージシャンについて知らなかった何かを知ることができた
かのようだった。ミュージック・ビデオが登場すると、こういった
部分がいくらか失われてしまったように思う。いまやアーティスト
についての重要な視覚的情報はビデオから得られるようになった。
しかし、アルバムの物言わぬイメージによってある種の神秘は可能だ。

『Tropicalia』では、軽さと明瞭さを表現することが重要だった。サウンド
はは飾り立てたものではなく、キーボードは明瞭で、音符は秩序を
持って配置されていた。ボサノバには本質的に官能的なインテリ
ジェンスがあるが、このことをイメージを通して伝達したかった。また、
曲が少しレトロであったため、60年代後半の科学の本のようなグラ
フィックとなった。

『Mutations』のジャケット写真は、ニューヨーク、バッファローのバック
ステージでの僕のスナップショットで、ドライクリーニングの袋を
かぶっている。表紙の写真撮影を何度も繰り返していたが、自然な
感じにならず、音楽の気楽さとスピリットが伝わってこなかった。
そこでガールフレンドのリーがこの写真に気がつき、これを使うべき
だと主張した。あまり良い写真とは思えなかったが、とにかくその案
を採用してみたところうまくいった（背景の衣装変え用のトレーラー
は切り取った）。

実際にどのようにアートワークを制作するのか。

アートワークは通常、写真、コラージュ、ドローイングから成り、コン
ピューターに取り込まれ、さまざまなグラフィックソフトによって
組み立てられる。『Odelay』のジャケットは、犬の本を参考にした
というだけのシンプルなものだった。色の修正はしたがそれだけだ。
中ページの方により手をかけている。僕は、デザイナーとともに何日も
コンピューターの前に座り、コラージュを創り上げた。多くのイメージ
をスキャナーで取り込み、切り刻んで操作し、全体の構成にたどり
ついた。この過程では多くの試みと失敗があった。時には、ひとつの
イメージを消し去って、残像のアウトラインをとった。一方で、僕は
ドローイングを進めながら、それをスキャンし、コラージュの上に
重ねていった。このようなプロセスは付加的で、レコーディングの方
法と似ていた。僕は、このイメージでカオスと色を表現すると同時に、
相互に関連のある流れをつくりたかった。

シングル『Tropicalia』では、僕がハサミとのりで手作業で創った
コラージュの一部を使用した。

ジャケット・デザインのクリエーターはどのように選ぶのか。

彼は、僕の所属するレコード・レーベルのスタッフだった。最初から
僕の担当で、3つのアルバムを一緒にやっている。

だれがロゴタイプをつくったのか。

僕はいつもタイポの本という本を取り寄せて、その中から好きな
ものを探す。そして、デザイナーにいくつかレイアウトしてもらい、
イメージにマッチするものを僕自身が選んでいる。トレンディな
タイポというものは常にあるが、意識して時代遅れのものを使う
ようにしている。『Odelay』のウェスタンなタイポは、音楽に対して
わざとらしいコントラストをもたらした。（曲のいくつかは、わざと
らしさのあるものだったと思うが。）『Mutations』では、僕たちは
タイポをゼロから創り上げていった。今では、これは必要なことと考え
ている。僕の新しいリリースはすべてオリジナルなタイポを使用
してる。

アートワークと音楽との関係は。

心と魂を注ぎ込んだ音楽にビジュアル・イメージをつけることは、
非常に重要な部分だからこそ難しい。イメージは、その音楽に対する
理解をみごとなまでに決定する。内在する音へ僕たちの欲望を刺激
する。イメージは永遠に音楽への視覚的リファレンスとなる。好きな
アルバムを思い浮かべる時、まず最初に心にフラッシュするのは
アルバムのアートワークだ。一流のアルバムはひとつのイベントで
あり、一文化を代表するものだ。ストーンズの新しいレコード・
リリースは、彼らの音楽と同じようにラウドなニュースとなった
だろう。ビートルズは、リボルバーとサージェント・ペッパーで彼らの
芸術的サウンドとパーソナリティを洗練させた。サウンドとイメージ
の密接な結合は造られたものではなく、より偶発的で直覚的なものだ。
僕がここで意味するのは、真にすばらしいイメージの結合のことだ。
僕自身の場合は、予定のジャケットを取り止めたこともしばしば
だったし、表面上はランダムに使用されたかのようだったが、時が経つ
につれ、結局は適当な選択であったと認められているようだ。『Odelay』
の場合、僕はまったくアイデアがなく、ジャケットが非常に遅れていた。

ところが、犬の本をパラパラとめくっている時、コモンドール犬が
ハードルを飛び越えている絵に出会った。このイメージはユーモア
にあふれ、しかも青い空とハードルの赤と白という原色使いが美的
にも心地よく、僕の心をとらえた。シンプルで直覚的なグラフィックの
クオリティはとても満足なものだった。それに、アルバム制作に1年
を費やしたことで、ちょうど僕自身がハードルを飛び越えたような
気持ちであったため、このイメージと自分とを結び付けた。現代の
アルバム・ジャケットを考える時、最も重要な要素はCDというサイズ
だと思う。このフォーマットに強要されるスペースの限界は、我々の
アプローチを大幅に変えることになった。このように小さな面には
それほど多くのことは表現できない。僕は、ひとつのジャケットに
ひとつの人物あるいは物までと決めている。多くても2つだ。この
制限のなかではできるだけシンプルにしなければならず、野心的
にもなれない。

逆に、中ページのアートワークのスペースは広がった。いまやイメージの
連続する小冊子となり、10〜12面の折り込みページになった。しかし、
まだこのサイズとフォーマットに対していろいろと試行錯誤している
と思う。このサイズで何が最もうまく表現できるのか。アプローチの
再考が必要だ。これらの制限を心にとめておくことは不可欠だ。僕の
アルバムでは、曲は全体としてひとつの集合体をつくる傾向がある
ため、折り込みページの形を使うことが多い。多様でありながら相互
に関係しあう、連続的なイメージの流れを創ることができるからだ。

ODELAY *BECK*

GEFFEN RECORDS 1996 USA GED24926
ART DIRECTION/DESIGN: BECK HANSEN & ROBERT FISHER   COVER PHOTO: LUDWIG
BECK PHOTOS: NITIN VADUKAL   INLAY PAINTING: MANUEL OCAMPO
COLLAGE IMAGES: AL HASEN, MANUEL OCAMPO, ZARIM OSBORN

front

techno
house
soul
rap

back

booklet

www.the-raft.com

LUNATIC HARNESS *μ-Ziq*
VIRGIN RECORDS 1997 UK ICPN724384430924

by permission from Astralwerks Records

BRACE YOURSELF *μ-Ziq*
ASTRALWERKS RECORDS 1998 USA ASW6235-2

booklet

case front

Resident.
Two years of Oakenfold at Cream.

VTDCDX 237
724384722821

**Resident.
CD one.**

**Resident.
CD two.**

TWO YEARS OF OAKENFOLD AT CREAM   *RESIDENT*

VIRGIN RECORDS   1999   UK   VTDCDX237   724384722821

sleeve back

THE K & D SESSIONS™ *KRUDER DORFMEISTER*
STUDIO-K7 RECORDS 1998 GERMANY K7073

THE FUTURE SOUND OF JAZZ VOL.3 *V.A.*
COMPOST RECORDS 1996 GERMANY CPT030-2
D: ANDREW ARNOLD (aa7@csi.com) DF: AA GRAPHIC DESIGN

front

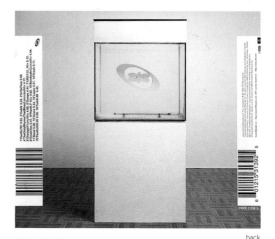

back

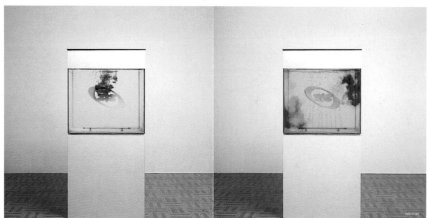

booklet

808:88:98   *808 STATE*

ZTT RECORDS   1998   UK   USD-53139

1999   *BINARY FINARY*
ORBIT RECORDS   1999   GERMANY   8 95664 2
AD, D, P, I: EIKE KOENIG   DF: EIKES GRAFISCHER HORT

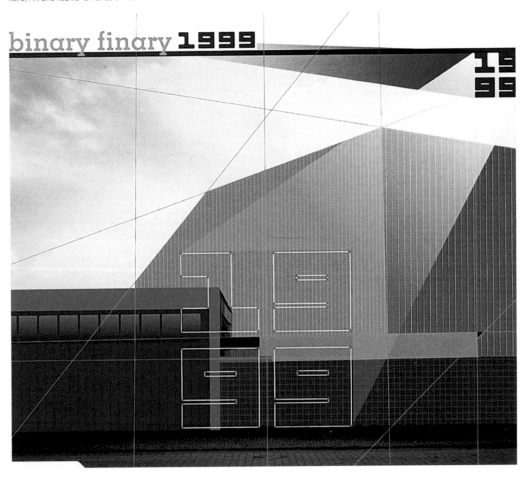

front

PARADISE   *FRIDGE*
ORBIT RECORDS   1999   GERMANY   8 95839 2
AD, D, P: EIKE KOENIG   DF: EIKES GRAFISCHER HORT

sleeve back

front

FRONT

case front

TRACKLISTING/S
[DISK Y/N: DEEP DARK, PHATT & INSANE] 01 BIG BANG 02 BANGING TRAFFIC [INTERLUDE] 03 LOVE IN TRAFFIC 04 DARKNESS 05 UP IN FLAMES 06 SNEAKY ONE
07 PROHIBITED ONE [INTERLUDE] 08 SECRET PLACE 09 FLUTE & FLAVA [DISK YANG: ANTICIPATION, INTENTION, HERITAGE & EVIDENCE] 01 INSPIRED
02 COME TO ME 03 HEAVEN 04 SINCERITY [PART 1 & 2] 05 COME TO ME [LAMENTO TAKE 2] 06 BLACK OPAL

RUN DISK 01	RUN DISK 02	ARTIST	TOTAL
0H42M29S	0H38M36S	SATOSHI TOMIIE:	1H21M05S
		FULL LICK	

TITLE:

CATALOGUE NUMBER
AICT 1067-8

DISK RELEASE
PUSH PLASTIC CASE
TO YOUR RIGHT

SPIRAL

CATALOGUE NUMBER
AICT1067-8
PAGE NUMBER
9

booklet

FULL LICK *SATOSHI TOMIIE*

SMEJ ASSOCIATED RECORDS 1999 JAPAN AICT1067-8
DF: THE DESIGNERS REPUBLIC

FUTURE JUJU *BLACK JAZZ CHRONICLES*

NUPHONIC RECORDS 1998 UK NUX121CD
D: TOM HINGSTON & ALYSON WALLER@TH STUDIO
P: ALEXANDER VAN BERGE COMMISSIONED BY: NUPHONIC RECORDS

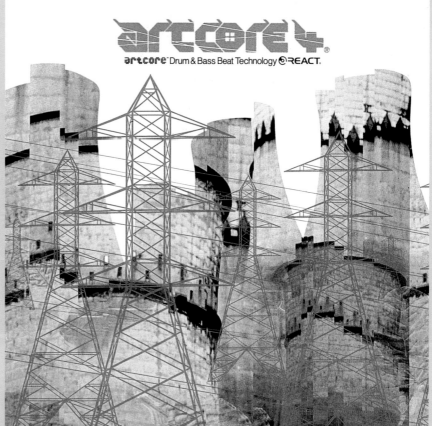

ARTCORE4 *V.A.*

REACT MUSIC 1997 UK REACTCD112
CD, AD, D, P, I, DF: THE DESIGNERS REPUBLIC

front

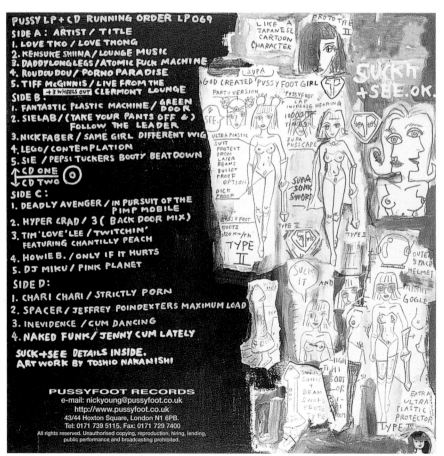

SUCK IT AND SEE *V.A.*

PUSSYFOOT RECORDS 1998 UK CDLPO69
CD, AD, D, I: TOSHIO NAKANISHI

back

booklet

front

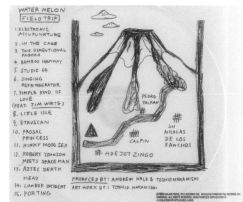

FIELD TRIP *WATER MELON*
FILE RECORDS 1999 JAPAN MFCD-067

back

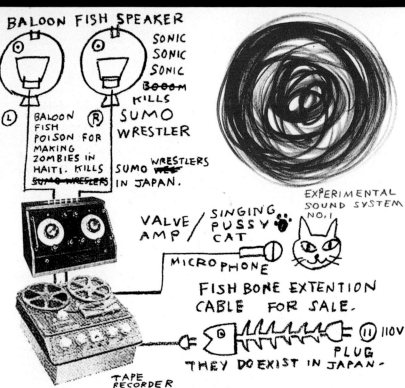

FISH SMELL LIKE CAT *V.A.*
PUSSYFOOT RECORDS 1997 UK LP005
CD, AD, D, I: TOSHIO NAKANISHI

jewel case   front

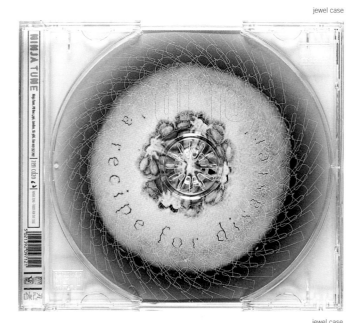

'a recipe for disaster'

jewel case   front

A RECIPE FOR DISASTER   *DJ FOOD*

NINJA TUNE 1995 UK ZENCD20
CD, AD, D, P, I, DF: OPENMIND

REFRIED FOOD   *DJ FOOD*

NINJA TUNE 1996 UK ZENCD21
CD, AD, D, P, I, DF: OPENMIND

SUNDAY BEST   *V.A.*

DUST2DUST 1999 UK SPECCD505
AD: JOSIE LYNWOODE

front

jewel case with disk

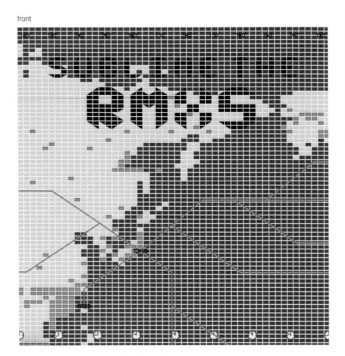

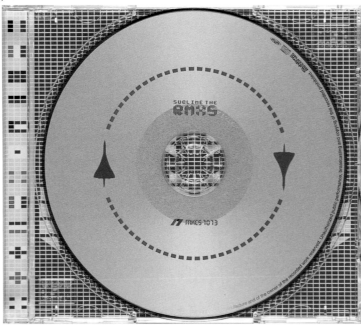

fold-out booklet

SUBLIME THE RMXS *V.A.*
SUBLIME RECORDS 1998 JAPAN MKCS1013

PAPERECORDINGSPLINTER *V.A.*
Ki/oon RECORDS 1998 JAPAN KSC3918

INDIVIDUAL ORCHESTRA *KARAFUTO*
Ki/oon RECORDS 1998 JAPAN KSC3912

front

BluPeter:Widescreen&Digital

inner

WIDESCREEN & DIGITAL *BLU PETER*
REACT MUSIC 1999 UK REACTCD146
CD, AD, D, P, DF: THE DESIGNERS REPUBLIC

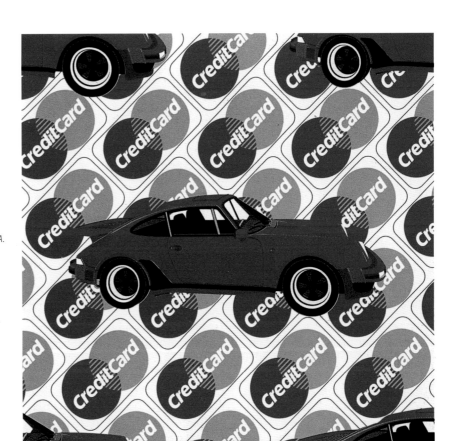

TRACK: FUNKELECTRIC *V.A.*
HYDROGEN DUKEBOX 1998 UK DUKE043CD
DF: YACHT ASSOCIATES

TRACK: FURTHERFUNK *V.A.*
HYDROGEN DUKEBOX 1998 UK DUKE050CD
DF: YACHT ASSOCIATES

front

KEN ISHII METAL BLUE AMERICA

All Songs Written and Produced by Ken Ishii.

℗1997 R & S Records. ©1997 Sony Music Entertainment
(Japan) Inc. Manufactured by Sony Music Entertainment
(Japan) Inc. R & S is a Trademark. (js) WARNING : All Rights
Reserved. Unauthorized duplication is a violation of applicable
laws. SonyTechno Page http://www.sme.co.jp/SonyTechno/
E-mail:techno@sme.co.jp   SRCS8523 STEREO

4 988009 852393

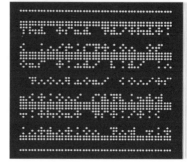

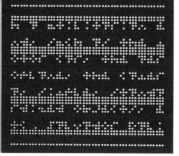

inner

メタル・ブルー・アメリカ METAL BLUE AMERICA   ケンイシイ KEN ISHII
SONY MUSIC ENTERTAINMENT（JAPAN） 1997 JAPAN SRCS8523

ORGANIC TECHNOLOJI '1998 *BOTCHIT AND SCARPER*

LASTRUM. CORPORATION 1998 JAPAN LACO-0009~0010

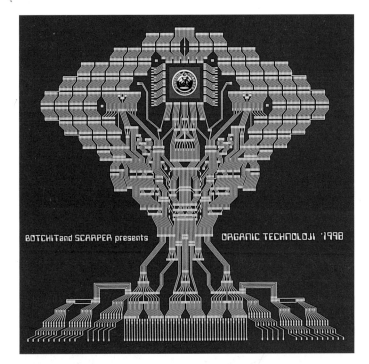

FUCKING CONSUMER *I-F*

DISKO B 1998 GERMANY DB69CD
CD, AD, D, P, I: ANDREAS DÖHRING

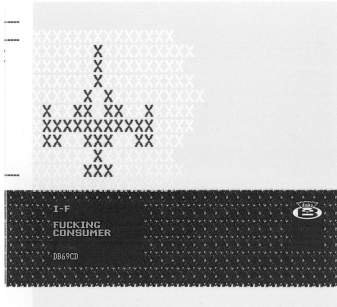

SYNTHESIS *KIRK DEGIORGIO*

X:TREME RECORDS 1998 UK XTR48CDM

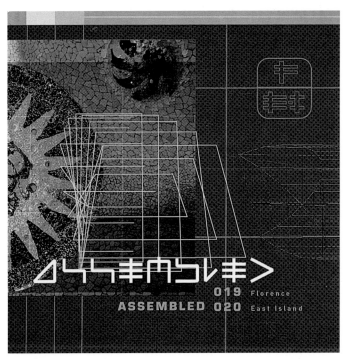

ASSEMBLED 019 / 020 *V.A.*

EEVO LUTE MUZIQUE 1996 THE NETHERLANDS EEVOCD6
CD, AD, D, P: J.J.F.G. BORRENBERGS DF: STOERE BINKEN DESIGN

front

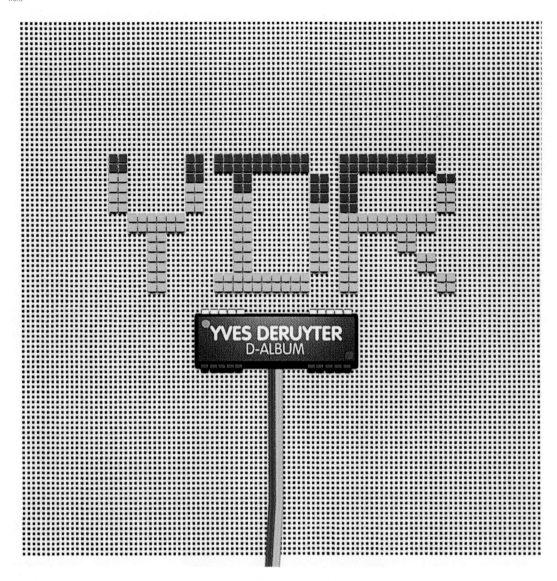

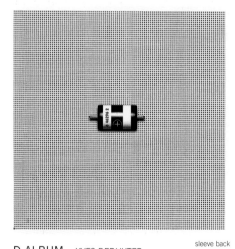

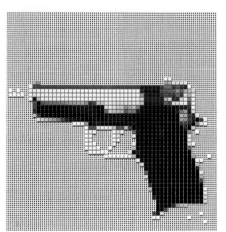

sleeve back

booklet

booklet

D-ALBUM *YVES DERUYTER*

ORBIT RECORDS 1998 GERMANY 8 46296 2
AD, D: EIKE KOENIG & RALF HIEMISCH P: BERND WESTPHAL
DE EIKES GRAFISCHER HORT

FLASHBACK DISCO 電気グルーヴ DENKI GROOVE
Ki/oon RECORDS 1999 JAPAN KSC2294

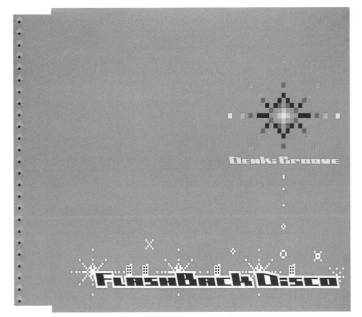

MICROSCOPIC SOUND V.A.
CAIPIRINHA MUSIC 1999 USA CAI2021
D: TAYLOR DEUPREE(12K) IMAGE: CARSTEN NICOLAI

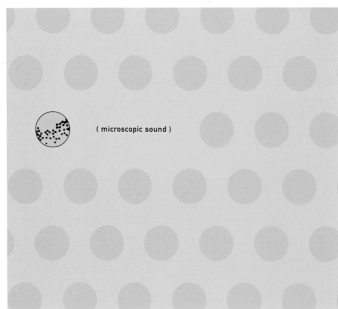

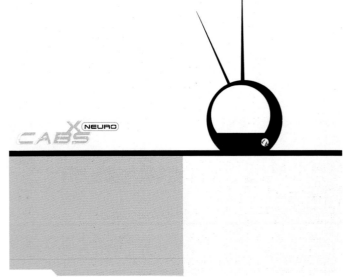

SYSTEM EXPRESS SYSTEM 7
FLAVOUR OF SOUND 1998 JAPAN TFCK-87591~2

NEURO X-CABS
ORBIT RECORDS 1996 GERMANY 8 93552 2
AD: EIKE KOENIG D, I: MARCO FIEDLER DF: EIKES GRAFISCHER HORT

**PETE TONG ESSENTIAL SELECTION
SPRING 1999** *V.A.*
ESSENTIAL RECORDINGS 1999 UK 556088.2
D: PETE MAUDER DF: MALARKEY (malarkey@dircon.co.uk)

**PETE TONG ESSENTIAL SELECTION
SUMMER 1998** *V.A.*
ESSENTIAL RECORDINGS 1998 UK 565961.2
D: PETE MAUDER DF: MALARKEY (malarkey@dircon.co.uk)

ALPHABET FLASHER   *DRUM KOMPUTER*

12K 1998 USA 12K1002
D: TAYLOR DEUPREE (12K)   TYPEFACE: DRUM KOMPUTER BY TAYLOR DEUPREE (CHANNELZERO!)

AMBIENT SYSTEMS 4   *V.A.*

INSTINCT RECORDS 1998 USA EX411
D: TAYLOR DEUPREE (12K)   ENGLISH TYPEFACE: SURGICAL ECHO BY ANDI JONES (CHANNELZERO!)

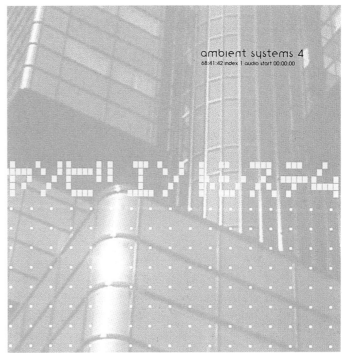

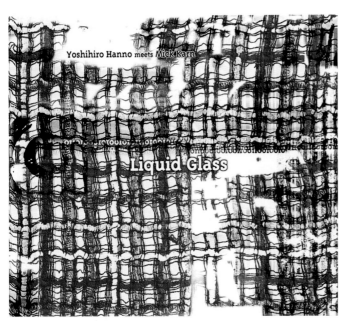

LIQUID GLASS   *YOSHIHIRO HANNO, MICK KARN*

FLAVOUR OF SOUND 1998 JAPAN TFCC-87582
ARTWORK: ARIAKI TSUJIMOTO, YOSHIHIRO HANNO (PICS AUDIO ARCHIVE)

PORTRAIT OF A POET   *YOSHIHIRO HANNO*

FLAVOUR OF SOUND 1998 JAPAN TFCC-87586
ARTWORK: ARIAKI TSUJIMOTO, YOSHIHIRO HANNO (PICS AUDIO ARCHIVE)   COVER PAINTING: KAORI HIRAO

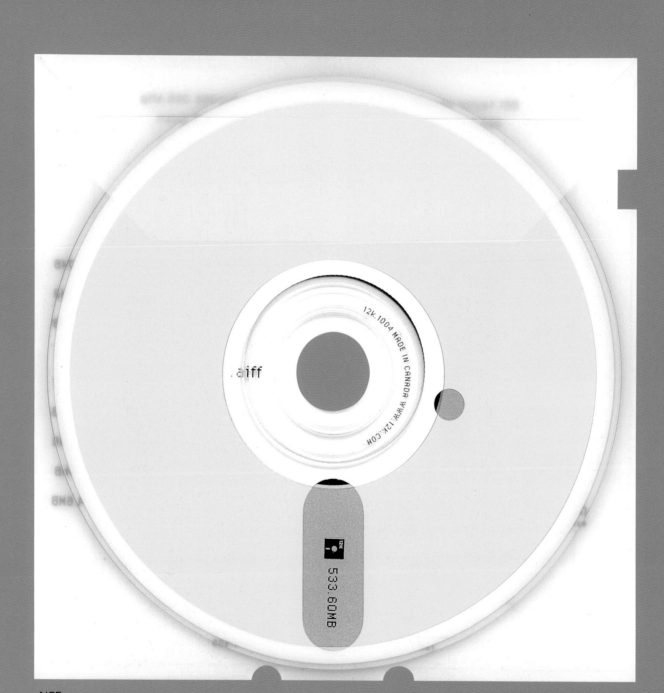

.AIFF *V.A.*

12K 1999 USA 12K1004
MYLAR LASER CUT AND DESIGN: DAN ABRAMS
DESIGN CONCEPT: TAYLOR DEUPREE (12K)

front

summer 97 <ali + basti> tiefschwarz ___ 01.
sweet mama <don olivier + m. mohr> ___ 02.
liquid combo
life love warm & leatherette remix ___ 03.
<thomas binder> implode
bahia blanca <toshi> oshmusic ___ 04.
soda stream <marc frank> ___ 05.
les copains des gammas.
double play <toshi> oshmusic ___ 06.
monte rosso <don olivier + a. scholl> ___ 07.
sonic sophistry
all of me <marc frank> carlo & marco ___ 08.
toshi's islànd <mischa> mischinski & frenkel ___ 09.
we fusion <ali + basti> tiefschwarz ___ 10.

back

PAULS=3 V.A.

PAULS BOUTIQUE 1998 GERMANY PB003
CD: OLIVER-A KRIMMEL, ANJA OSTERWALDER DF: I_D BÜRO

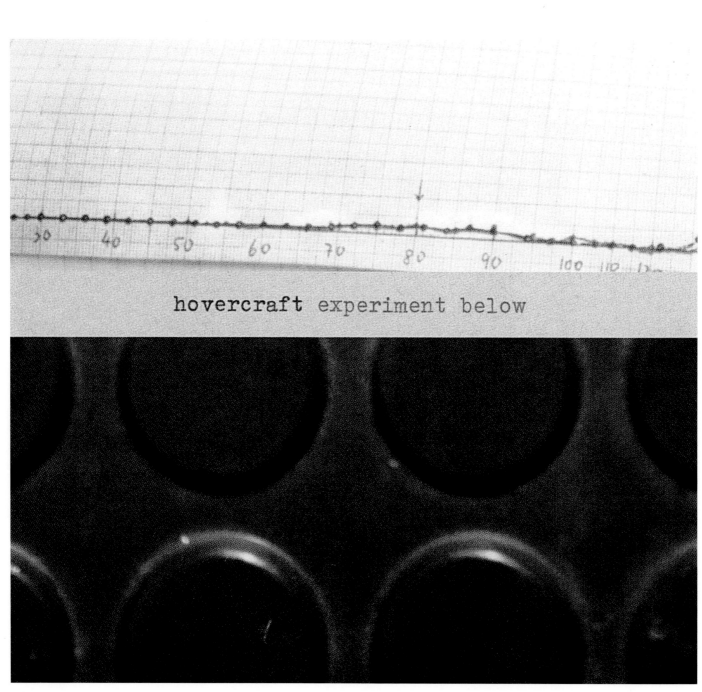

hovercraft experiment below

EXPERIMENT BELOW *HOVERCRAFT*
MUTE / BLAST FIRST 1998 UK BFFP160CD

STATISTICS *BIO ELECTRONICS*
RAMP RECORDS 1999 GERMANY
CD: OLIVER-A KRIMMEL, ANJA OSTERWALDER D: FRANK ZUBER P: I_D TEAM DF: I_D BÜRO

HOTEI BATTLE ROYAL MIXES II *V.A.*
TOSHIBA EMI 1998 JAPAN TOCT-10278
AD: 立花 ハジメ HAJIME TACHIBANA D: 原 圭吾 KEIGO HARA
DF: 立花ハジメデザイン HAJIME TACHIBANA DESIGN

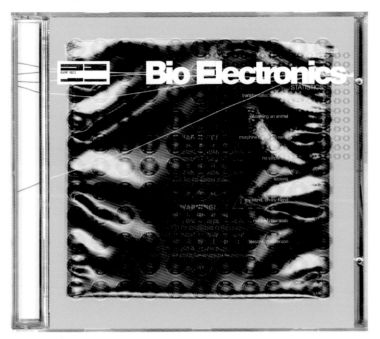

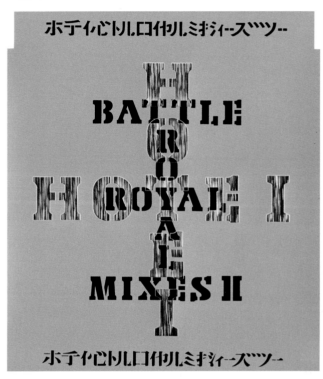

front

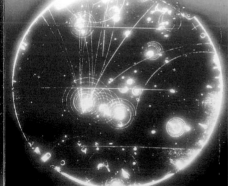

inner

BALANCE OF THE FORCE
BOYMERANG
REGAL RECORDINGS 1997 UK 7243 8 56610 2 0

front

disk

TAKAGIKAN HELLO

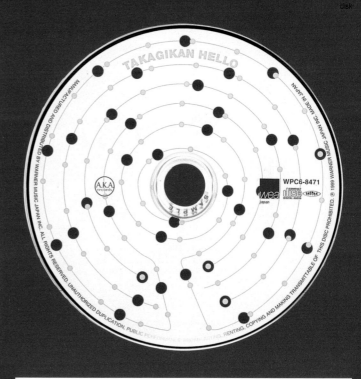

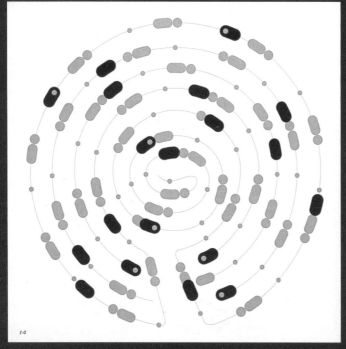

14

8

booklet

booklet

HELLO *TAKAGIKAN*
WARNER MUSIC JAPAN 1999 JAPAN WPC6-8471
AD, D: 立花 ハジメ HAJIME TACHIBANA DF: 立花ハジメデザイン HAJIME TACHIBANA DESIGN

front

a certain frank

nobody ? no !

disk

NOBODY ? NO !   *A CERTAIN FRANK*

ATA TAK 1998 GERMANY 03771-2

NEW FORMS *RONI SIZE REPRAZENT*
MERCURY 1997 UK TALKIN' LOUD534 933-2

21ST CENTURY SOUL *V.A.*
MERCURY 1997 UK 534 742-2

THE TUNNEL *THE M.EXPERIENCE*

ORBIT RECORDS   1999   GERMANY   8 95705 2
AD, D, P: EIKE KOENIG   DF: EIKES GRAFISCHER HORT

front   sleeve back

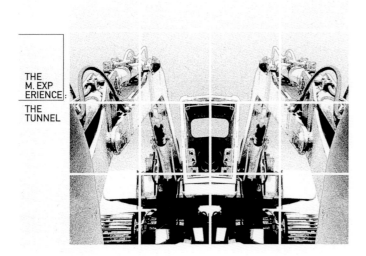

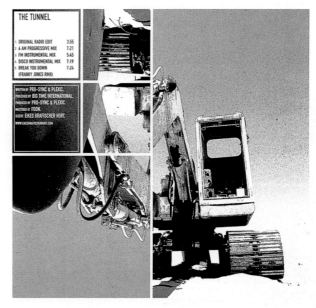

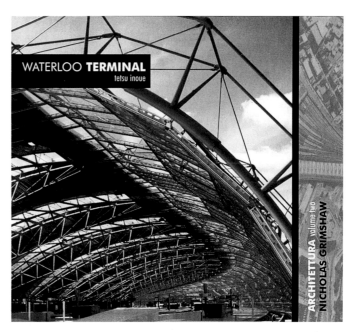

LISTEN AND FLY *V.A.*

PAULS MUSIQUE   1999   GERMANY
CD: OLIVER-A KRIMMEL, ANJA OSTERWALDER   D: FRANK ZUBER   P: I_D TEAM   DF: I_D BÜRO

WATERLOO TERMINAL *TETSU INOUE*

CAIPIRINHA MUSIC   1998   USA   CAI2015
D: TAYLOR DEUPREE (12K)

BEAUCOUP FISH *UNDERWORLD*
JBO / V2 MUSIC 1998 UK JBO1005438
D: TOMATO

PUSH UPSTAIRS *UNDERWORLD*
JBO / V2 MUSIC 1998 UK JBO05005440
D: TOMATO

FUTURE SOUL 003 *V.A.*
SMEJ ASSOCIATED RECORDS 1999 JAPAN AICT54~55
DF: TGB DESIGN

front

sleeve back

©1999 Sony Music Entertainment (Japan) Inc. Manufactured by Sony Music Entertainment (Japan) Inc. is a Trademark of Sony Music Entertainment (Japan) Inc. (yp)
WARNING : All Rights Reserved. Unauthorized duplication is a violation of applicable laws.
AICT 54~55 / STEREO

front

booklet

BVCP-21029

DEEP DISH *JUNK SCIENCE*
BMG FUNHOUSE 1998 JAPAN BVCP-21029 (74321-58034-2)

MUSIC FOR LIVING SOUND Cool Sounds From Real Life
YANN TOMITA
FOR LIFE 1998 JAPAN FLCF-3715
ARTWORK: YANN TOMITA

box front

front

front

disk

MODULATION & TRANSFORMATION 4 *V.A.*

MILLE PLATEAUX 1999 GERMANY MP3CD61
AD, D: PETER WEINHEIMER DF: MILLE PLATEAUX

ISO FABRIC *OVAL*
TOKUMA JAPAN COMMUNICATIONS 1997 JAPAN TKCB-71277

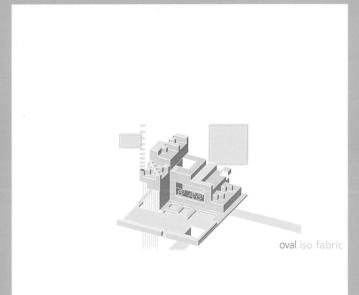

SN-DING *MICROSTORIA*
TOKUMA JAPAN COMMUNICATIONS 1994-1996 JAPAN TKCB-71276

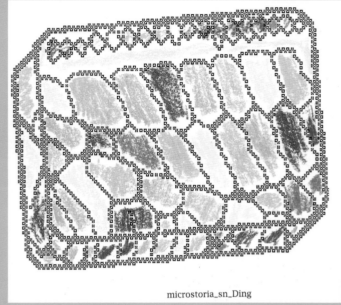

inner

front

AERO DEKO EP *OVAL*
TOKUMA JAPAN COMMUNICATIONS 1998 JAPAN TKCB-71463

ORGANISM *JIMI TENOR*
WARP RECORDS 1999 UK WARPCD60

MUSICA NOVA *MUSICA NOVA*

ns-com 1997 JAPAN LIN-CD001
DF: TGB DESIGN

SOUNDS FROM THE ELECTRONIC LOUNGE *V.A.*

REACT MUSIC 1998 UK REACTCD123
CD, AD, D, I, DF: THE DESIGNERS REPUBLIC P: CHARLIE DAAS

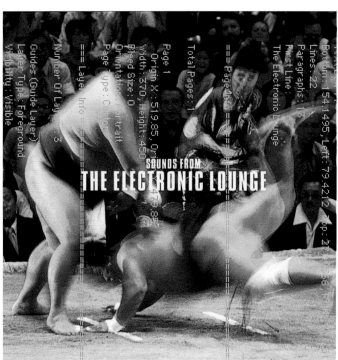

USUAL THINGS *LITTLE TEMPO*

cutting edge 1999 JAPAN CTCR-11052
AD: SEIJI "BIG BIRD"

こどもと魔法 CHILD AND MAGIC *竹村 延和 NOBUKAZU TAKEMURA*

WARNER MUSIC JAPAN 1997 JAPAN WPC6-8399
AD, D: 小野 英作 EISAKU ONO（NANA） I: 伊藤 桂司 KEIJI ITO

ELECTRIC MUSIC *ELECTRIC MUSIC*
NIPPON CROWN 1998 JAPAN CRCL-4704
D: 井上 幹也 MIKIYA INOUE

HEMISPHERE *HEMISPHERE*
QUANTUM LOOP RECORDS 1998 CANADA 001
AD, D: STEPHEN PARKES   D: TROY BAILLY   DF: PROTOTYPE DESIGN

TRANSIENT DAWN *V.A.*
TRANSIENT RECORDS 1997 UK TRANR609CD
CD, AD, D, I: RIAN HUGHES DF: DEVICE

OPEN SKIES *V.A.*
TRANSIENT RECORDS 1999 UK TRANR624CD
CD, AD, D: RIAN HUGHES DF: DEVICE

LIKE WEATHER *LEILA*
REPHLEX 1998 UK CAT056CD
D: BOB, ROBIN, LEILA

front

back

AROUND THE HOUSE *HERBERT*
PHONOGRAPHY 1998 UK GRAPHCD01
CD: MATTHEW HERBERT AD: CHRISTOPHER LEWIS COGHLAN D, I: SARAH HOPPER P: ANDY WALKER

WINDOWLICKER *APHEX TWIN*
WARP RECORDS 1999 UK WARP/SIRE35007-2

front

COME TO DADDY *APHEX TWIN*
WARP RECORDS 1997 UK WAP94CDX

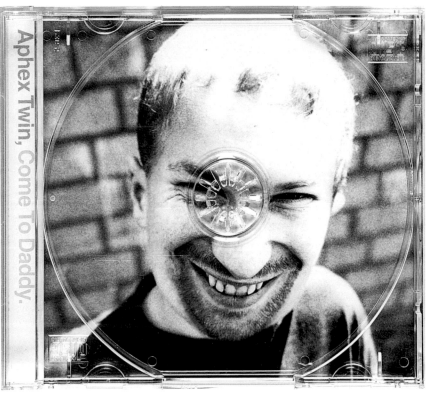

jewel case

HARD NORMAL DADDY *SQUAREPUSHER*

fold-out booklet

SONY MUSIC ENTERTAINMENT (JAPAN) 1997 JAPAN SRCS8260

REACTIVATE CLASSICS *V.A.*
REACT MUSIC 1998 UK REACTCDX114
CD, AD, D, I, DF: THE DESIGNERS REPUBLIC

PLATIPUS RECORDS VOLUME TWO *V.A.*
PLATIPUS RECORDS 1995 UK PLAT20CD
D: MARK NEAL DF: DUST DESIGN

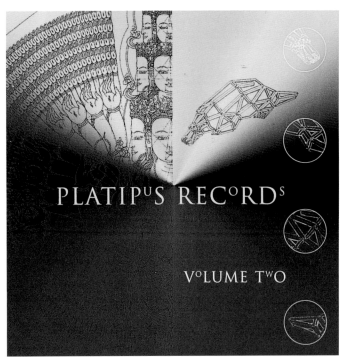

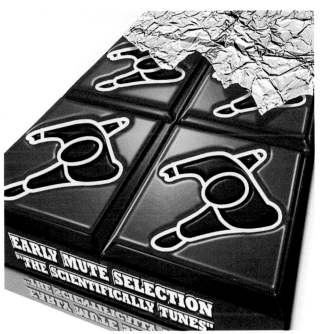

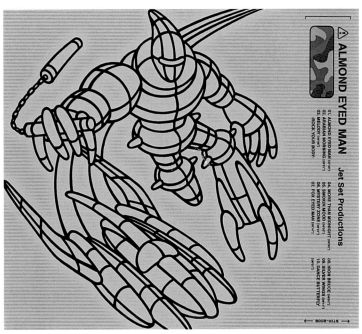

EARLY MUTE SELECTION
"THE SCIENTIFICALLY TUNES" *V.A.*

TOSHIBA EMI 1998 JAPAN TOCT-24016

ALMOND EYED MAN *JET SET PRODUCTIONS*

STATIC / INPARTMAINT 1999 JAPAN STIP-2008
D: SATOSHI OMIYA (MOP DESIGN) I: AKI AMEMIYA

STR8UP BREAKS *DJ CZECH*

DOSE PRODUCTIONS 1999 CANADA FF-001
CD, I: STEPHEN PARKES AD: DAVID PAPINEAU, TROY BAILLY
I: DAVID DENOFREO DF: PROTOTYPE DESIGN

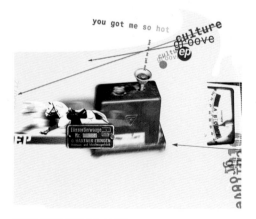

EMMA HOUSE 3 *V.A.*

cutting edge 1997 JAPAN CTCR-13100/1

HOUZE MUZIQUE *CELVIN ROTANE*

ORBIT RECORDS 1999 GERMANY 8 95917 2
AD, D, P: EIKE KOENIG & RALF HIEMISCH DF: EIKES GRAFISCHER HORT

YOU GOT ME SO HOT *CULTURE GROOVE EP*

ORBIT RECORDS 1996 GERMANY 8 93671 2
AD, D, P, I: EIKE KOENIG DF: EIKES GRAFISCHER HORT

FENG SHUI *Q-BURNS ABSTRACT MESSAGE*
ASTRALWERKS RECORDS 1998 USA ASW6228

by permission from Astralwerks Records

OUT OF BODY SESSIONS *WATER MELON*
FILE RECORDS 1997 JAPAN MFCD-064

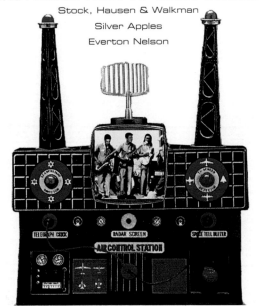

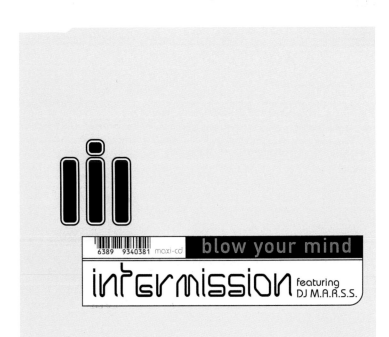

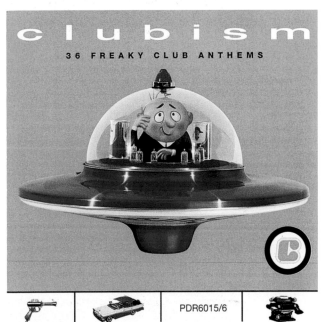

BLOW YOUR MIND *INTERMISSION FEAT. DJ M.A.R.S.S.*
INTERCORD 1997 GERMANY BLOW UP INT8 84581 2
CD: OLIVER-A KRIMMEL, ANJA OSTERWALDER DF: I_D BÜRO

CLUBISM *36 FREAKY CLUB ANTHEMS*
MS TRADING / DIFFERENT DANCE RECORDS 1997 BELGIUM PDR6015/6
CD, AD, D: SVEN MASTBOOMS P: STOCK DF: SEVEN PRODUCTIONS

inner

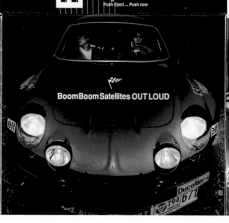

Boom Boom Satellites OUT LOUD

MissingNote/07:02,Batter The Jam No.3/05:59, PushEject/05:28,Limbo/07:30,Intruder/01:10,An Owl/04:36,Oneness/02:35,Scatterin'Monkey/05:14,Def/04:10,OnThe PaintedDesert/08:35

case front

front

OUT LOUD *BOOM BOOM SATELLITES*

SONY MUSIC ENTERTAINMENT (JAPAN) 1998 JAPAN RS99149CDX

ALL AREAS *V.A.*

VISION-MUSIC 1999 GERMANY
CD: OLIVER-A KRIMMEL, ANJA OSTERWALDER D: STEFAN WALZ P: I_D TEAM DF: I_D BÜRO

A STREETCAR NAMED DESIRE *V.A.*

MALAUSCHEK 1999 GERMANY
CD: OLIVER-A KRIMMEL, ANJA OSTERWALDER P: I_D TEAM DF: I_D BÜRO

1999 MCA Records, Inc. by arrangement with TWISTED. All Rights Reserved. Artwork reproduced by kind permission.

BANG LIBÉRATION *FUNKY DERRICK*

TWISTED America Records 1998 USA TWDM-55495
CD, AD, D, I: STEVEN NEWMAN P: KARIN ROISSEAUX DF: COMPRESSION STUDIOS

FREE STYLE *GILLES PETERSON / TALKIN' LOUD*

MERCURY 1998 JAPAN PHCR-1633
AD, D: 角田 純一 JUNICHI TSUNODA D: 石黒 景太 KEITA ISHIGURO DF: ㈲マナス MANAS INC.

front

booklet

back

RO 3003 *V.A.*

BUNGALOW 1997 GERMANY BUNG021

booklet

front

disk

THE SOUND OF '70S *YOSHINORI SUNAHARA*

Ki/oon RECORDS 1998 JAPAN KSC2243

front

artist: si begg title: commuter world   CAI2014-2

back

1	0.00	Good Morning
2	2.25	Commuter World (Baker Street)
3	7.38	Rush Hour Arrival (Oxford Circus)
4	9.08	Office Politics
5	15.06	R.S.I. and M.E. (Nineties Disease)
6	18.24	Like You Just Don't Care (Bored at Club U.K)
7	23.32	Journey Home (NCP to A40 Westbound)
8	24.23	All Night Session (Ruislip Manor)
9	29.45	I Was There (Sleep Deprivation)
10	31.05	24hr Garage Mission
11	34.33	Walk Home Through Shoe Box Estate
12	38.50	Post Jack Journey
13	44.52	Wave Station Platform 3
14	51.25	Delays on the Met Line
15	52.28	Signal Failure
16	56.29	Viaduct Route at Sunset
17	1.01.15	Living in Suburbia
18	1.05.51	Living in Suburbia pt 2
19	1.08.41	So Many People, So Little Noise

CAIPIRINHA MUSIC
caipirinha productions 1120 5th ave. #15a
new york, new york 10128
fax: 212.987.8940 www.caipirinha.com
distributed in the USA by Sire Records Group

artist: si begg title: commuter world

6 35407 20142 4

design by taylor deupree

starring, in order of appearance:

Si Begg
Fran Littlewood
Jess White
Anthony Alexander
Pete Finlay
Dezric Pendrummond
various cellar boys
a cast of thousands commuting into central London

published by Copyright Control

SUBURB: residential district situated on the outskirts of a city or town.
COMMUTE: 1. to travel some distance regularly. 2. to change.

06.ZONE7.TRANSFER.ASTOPB.CONNECT
see inlay for track locations

si begg: commuter world
CAIPIRINHA MUSIC
CAI2014

inner

COMMUTER WORLD   *SI BEGG*

CAIPIRINHA MUSIC 1998 USA CAI2014
D: TAYLOR DEUPREE (12K)

front

back

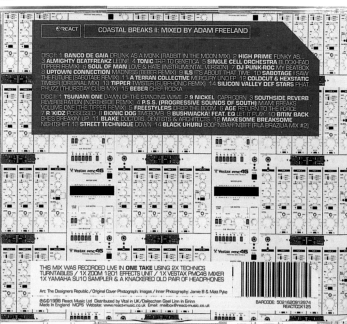

inner

COASTAL BREAKS II: MIXED BY ADAM FREELAND *V.A.*

REACT MUSIC 1998 UK REACTCDX125
CD, AD, D, DF: THE DESIGNERS REPUBLIC P: IMAGES

www.the-raft.com/massive

MEZZANINE   *MASSIVE ATTACK*
VIRGIN RECORDS 1998 UK VJCP-25360

ANGEL   *MASSIVE ATTACK*
VIRGIN RECORDS 1998 UK WBRX10

www.the-raft.com/massive

THE FAT OF THE LAND   *PRODIGY*
avex trax 1997 JAPAN AVCM-65020

DRIVE *GEARWHORE*
VIRGIN RECORDS 1998 UK CDASW6240 7243 8 47012 2 2

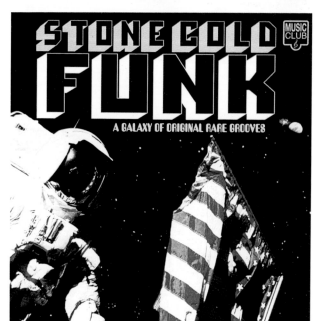

STONE COLD FUNK *V.A.*
MUSIC COLLECTION 1998 UK MCCD337

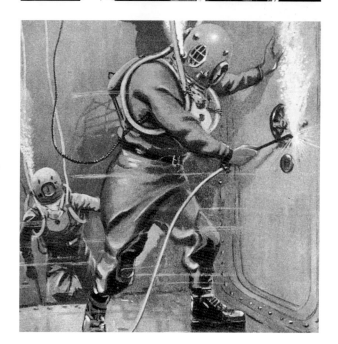

STAY DOWN *TWO LONE SWORDSMEN*
WARP RECORDS 1998 UK WARPCD58

techno house soul rap

MY LEFT PUSSYFOOT *V.A.*
PUSSYFOOT RECORDS 1999 UK CDLP013
CD, AD, D, I: KATE HARRISON (kateh@pussyfoot.co.uk)

MUY RICO! *JACKNIFE LEE*
PUSSYFOOT RECORDS 1999 UK CDLP017
CD, AD, D, I: KATE HARRISON (kateh@pussyfoot.co.uk)

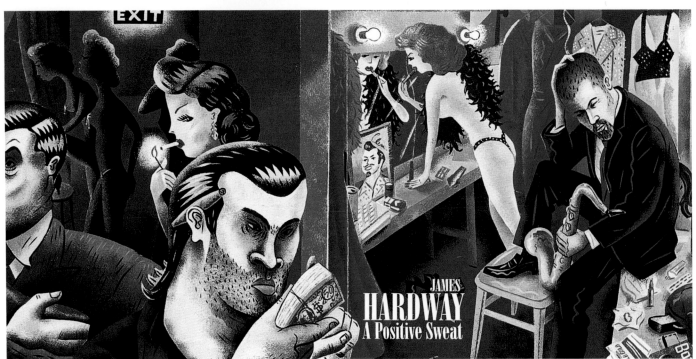

A POSITIVE SWEAT *JAMES HARDWAY*
HYDROGEN DUKEBOX / ROS 1999 UK HEMP28CDX
I: MARK McCONNEL DF: TOY BOX

sleeve back

front

SACREBLEU *DIMITRI FROM PARIS*
EAST WEST JAPAN 1997 JAPAN AMCE2364
AD, D: TOWA TEI & TYCOON GRAPHICS I: YUTAMPO SHIRANE

BRIMFUL OF ASHA *CORNERSHOP*
LUAKA BOP 1998 USA WIJ81CD

front

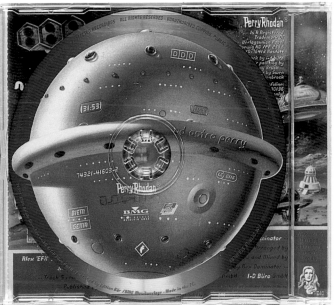

back

AD ASTRA PERRY *U·S·P*
BMG ARIOLA MÜNCHEN 1996 GERMANY 74321 41603-2
CD: OLIVER-A KRIMMEL, ANJA OSTERWALDER I: JONNY BRUCK DF: I_D BÜRO

front

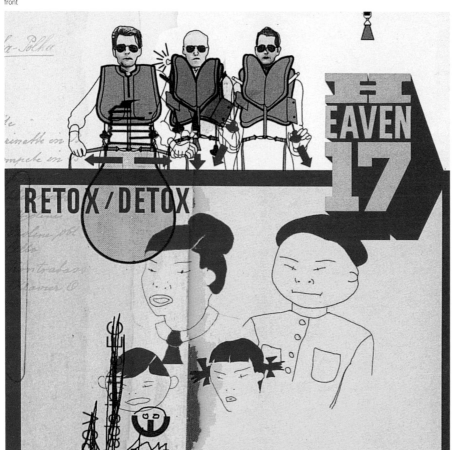

RETOX / DETOX *HEAVEN 17*
EAGLE RECORDS 1998 GERMANY EDLEAG094-2
AD, D, I: EIKE KOENIG P: GABY GERSTER (BOOKLET INSIDE)
I: RALF HIEMISCH, ALEK MANDRYSCH DF: EIKES GRAFISCHER HORT

jewel case with disk

booklet

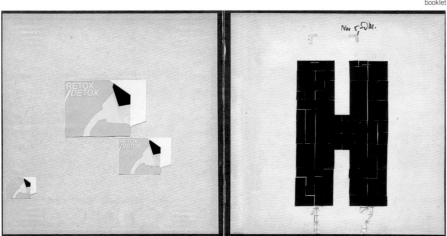

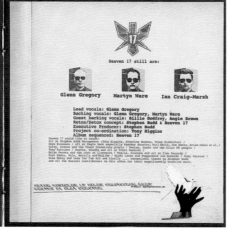

WITH THIS RING LET ME GO
MOLELLA & PHIL JAY PRESENT HEAVEN 17 MEETS FAST EDDIE
ORBIT RECORDS 1998 GERMANY 8 95101 2
AD, D: EIKE KOENIG AD, I: RALF HIEMISCH P: GABY GERSTER DF: EIKES GRAFISCHER HORT

SMILE *PAFFENDORF*
ORBIT RECORDS 1998 GERMANY 8 95210 2
AD, D: EIKE KOENIG AD, I: RALF HIEMISCH DF: EIKES GRAFISCHER HORT

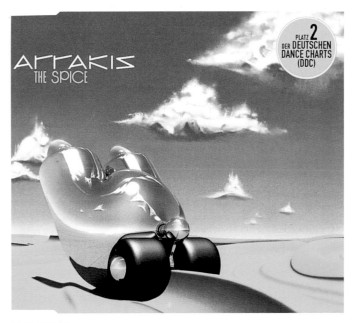

OPEN THE GATE / IRON EDEN *GATE*
ORBIT RECORDS 1998 GERMANY 8 95149 2
AD, D: EIKE KOENIG AD, I: RALF HIEMISCH DF: EIKES GRAFISCHER HORT

THE SPICE *ARRAKIS*
ORBIT RECORDS 1999 GERMANY 8 95727 2
AD, D: EIKE KOENIG AD, I: RALF HIEMISCH DF: EIKES GRAFISCHER HORT

SACRÉ FRANÇAIS   *DIMITRI FROM PARIS*

EAST WEST FRANCE 1997 FRANCE 3984 20121-2

ROC IN IT   *DEEJAY PUNK-ROC VS ONYX*

INDEPENDIENTE 1998 UK ISOM21MS
D: TRACY WORRALL

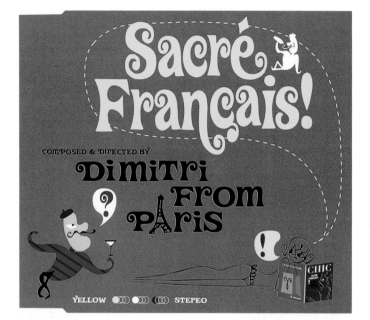

www.the-raft.com/wagonchrist

TALLY HO!   *WAGON CHRIST*

VIRGIN RECORDS 1998 UK CDV2863

HAZEL   *LOOP DA LOOP*

MERCURY 1999 UK FESCD53/566 799-2

MOONSHINE *COSMOSIS*

TRANSIENT RECORDS 1997 UK TRA034CD
CD, AD, D: RIAN HUGHES DF: DEVICE

TRANSIENT 6 *V.A.*

TRANSIENT RECORDS 1998 UK TRANR613CD
CD, AD, D: RIAN HUGHES DF: DEVICE

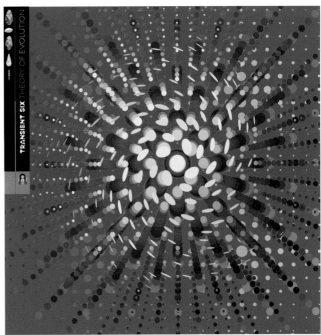

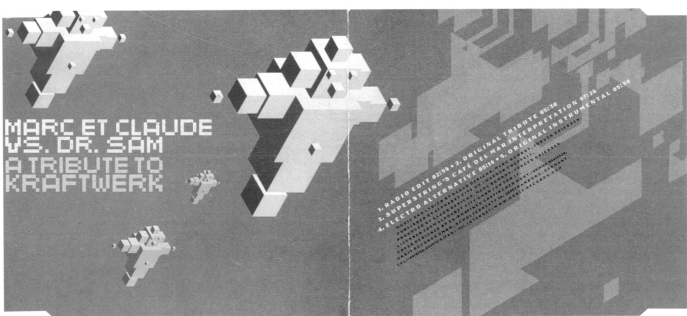

front

back

A TRIBUTE TO KRAFTWERK
MARC ET CLAUDE VS. DR. SAM

ORBIT RECORDS 1998 GERMANY 8 95315 2
AD, D, I: EIKE KOENIG DF: EIKES GRAFISCHER HORT

front

SOURCE ROCKS *V.A.*

SOURCE 1998 FRANCE 7243 8466112 0
P: BERNARD ANTKOWIAK WITH JÉROME COCHE
LITTLE DRUM SET: LAURENT BAUDOUX ARTWORK: FRANK LORIOU

jewel case

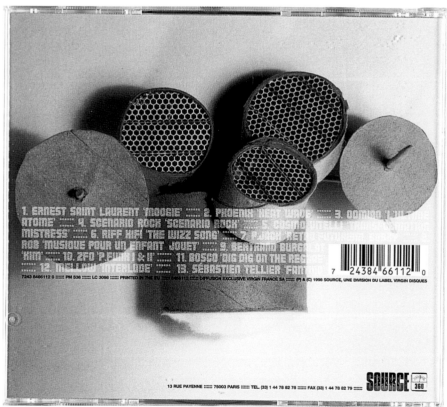

1. ERNEST SAINT LAURENT 'MOOGIE' :::::: 2. PHOENIX 'HEAT WAVE' :::::: 3. OOMIDO 'L'ULTIME ATOME' :::::: 4. SCENARIO ROCK 'SCENARIO ROCK' :::::: 5. COSMO VITELLI 'TRANSFORMATION MISTRESS' :::::: 6. RIFF HIFI 'THE WIZZ SONG' :::::: 7. P.JACK 'RETRO FUTURISM' :::::: 8. ROB 'MUSIQUE POUR UN ENFANT JOUET' :::::: 9. BERTRAND BURGALAT 'KIM' :::::: 10. 2FO 'P FUNK I & II' :::::: 11. BOSCO 'DIG DIG ON THE REGGAE' :::::: 12. MELLOW 'INTERLUDE' :::::: 13. SÉBASTIEN TELLIER 'FANTINO'

7243 8466112 0 :::::: PM 538 :::::: LC 3098 :::::: PRINTED IN THE EU 8466112 :::::: DIFFUSION EXCLUSIVE VIRGIN FRANCE SA :::::: (P) & (C) 1998 SOURCE, UNE DIVISION DU LABEL VIRGIN DISQUES

7 24384 66112 0

13 RUE PAYENNE :::::: 75003 PARIS :::::: TEL. (33) 1 44 78 82 78 :::::: FAX (33) 1 44 78 82 79

SOURCE 360

back

front

LOGIC TRANCE 3 *DJ DAG*

LOGIC RECORDS 1998 GERMANY 743 215 4727-2
AD, D, I: EIKE KOENIG DF: EIKES GRAFISCHER HORT

back

LIFESIGNS *RODD-Y-LER*

ORBIT RECORDS 1998 GERMANY 8 95012 2
AD, D: EIKE KOENIG DF: EIKES GRAFISCHER HORT

VARIOUS 12" *V.A.*

AUTOMATIC RECORDS 1998 UK AUTO12+
CD, AD, D: RIAN HUGHES DF: DEVICE

back   front

✮A **ORGAN-IC ORIGINAL MIX** not previously available ✮B **ONE TIME HALF FAT REMIX**
not previously available · original available on eve 5 ✮C **ON A DEEP TIP FOLLOW THE**
RIMSHOT REMIX not previously available · original available on eve 5 ✮D **THE STRANGER**
DAVID CRAIG REMIX previously available on eve 10 · original available on eve 6 ✮E **GRAND**
HALL ORIGINAL MIX not previously available ✮F1 **LORD OF THE UNIVERSE THE**
MOVING REMIX not previously available · original available on eve 11 ✮F2 **DEFINITION OF A**
TRACK DAVID CRAIG REMIX previously available on eve 10 · original available on eve 2

TRACKS B, C, D, F1 AND F2 © 1996 EVE RECORDS. TRACKS A AND E © AND © 1997 EVE RECORDS. EVE RECORDS U. K. TELEPHONE AND FAX (0171) 978 7878.
8 KINGFISHER COURT, 240 FALCON ROAD, LONDON SW11 U. K. EEE@EVE-RECORDS.CO.UK. E-MAIL STEVE@EVE-RECORDS.CO.UK. DISTRIBUTED BY FLING RECORDS
U. K. TELEPHONE 0385 743 7708 FAX 0385 743 7666. ORIGINAL COVER IMAGE TAKEN FROM A PAINTING BY SANTA ARRE. ALL RIGHTS RESERVED.
©2661 ITALY. DESIGNED BY RIAN "PARELITE" HUGHES AT DEVICE (0171) 221 9580. SET IN CORTONA, A DEVICE ORIGINAL FONT. EVE/97001. MADE IN THE U. K.

SENVA VOLTO   *PABLO GARGANO*

EVE RECORDS 1997 UK EVECD97001
CD, AD, D: RIAN HUGHES I: SANTA ARRE DF: DEVICE

back   front

SUNSHINE *KAY CEE*
ORBIT RECORDS 1999 GERMANY 8 97328 2
AD, D: EIKE KOENIG DF: EIKES GRAFISCHER HORT

MRS WOOD *JOANNA*
ORBIT RECORDS 1997 GERMANY 8 94467 2
AD, D, I: EIKE KOENIG DF: EIKES GRAFISCHER HORT

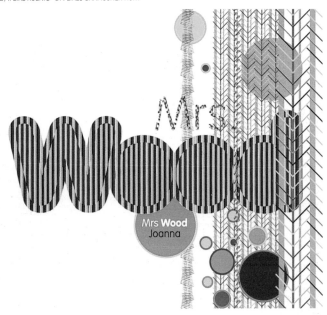

LUVSTRUCK *SOUTHSIDE SPINNERS*
ORBIT RECORDS 1999 GERMANY 8 96011 2
AD, D, P: EIKE KOENIG AD, I: RALF HIEMISCH DF: EIKES GRAFISCHER HORT

TRANCE EMOTIONS *U.S.U.R.A.*
ORBIT RECORDS 1998 GERMANY 8 94978 2
AD, D: EIKE KOENIG AD, D, I: RALF HIEMISCH P: BERND WESTPHAL DF: EIKES GRAFISCHER HORT

UNI UMIT *LITHOPS*
TOKUMA JAPAN COMMUNICATIONS 1998 JAPAN TKCB-71406

MOUSE ON MARS *GLAM*
TOKUMA JAPAN COMMUNICATIONS 1998 JAPAN TKCB-71440

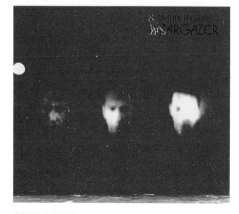

STARGAZER *BRANDI IFGRAY*
SÄHKÖ RECORDINGS 1999 FINLAND PUU-16
CD, AD, D: TOMMI GRÖNLUND P: VERTTI TERÄSVUORI DF: SÄHKÖ

TULKINTA *ø*
SÄHKÖ RECORDINGS 1997 FINLAND 13CD
CD, AD, D: TOMMI GRÖNLUND P: MARKO VUOKOLA DF: SÄHKÖ

LE MUTANT *BRANDI IFGRAY*

SÄHKÖ RECORDINGS 1996 FINLAND PUU6CD
CD, AD, D: TOMMI GRÖNLUND P: THRON ULLBERG DF: SÄHKÖ

front   back

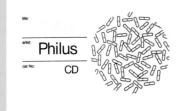

TETRA *PHILUS*

SÄHKÖ RECORDINGS 1997 FINLAND 15CD
CD, AD, D: TOMMI GRÖNLUND DF: SÄHKÖ

THE REMIXES *NUYORICAN SOUL*

cutting edge 1998 JAPAN CTCR13110

THE BEST OF THE ACID JAZZ YEARS *MOTHER EARTH*

PONY CANYON (ACID JAZZ) 1999 JAPAN PCCY01345
D: 松村 麻有美 MAYUMI MATSUMURA

BLOW UP! A JTQ COLLECTION *THE JAMES TAYLOR QUARTET*

MUSIC COLLECTION 1998 UK MCCD333

THE LATIN ONE *V.A.*

WESTSIDE 1999 UK WESM545
D: JAFFA DF: UNKNOWN

JAZZ ACID *V.A.*

WESTSIDE 1998 UK WESM557
D: JAFFA DF: UNKNOWN

ACID JAZZ MEETS FREE SOUL *V.A.*

PONY CANYON (ACID JAZZ) 1998 JAPAN PCCY01234
D: 栗原 聰 SATOSHI KURIHARA

jewel case with disk

front

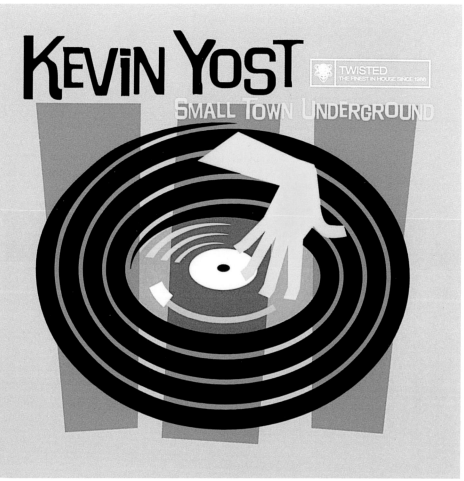

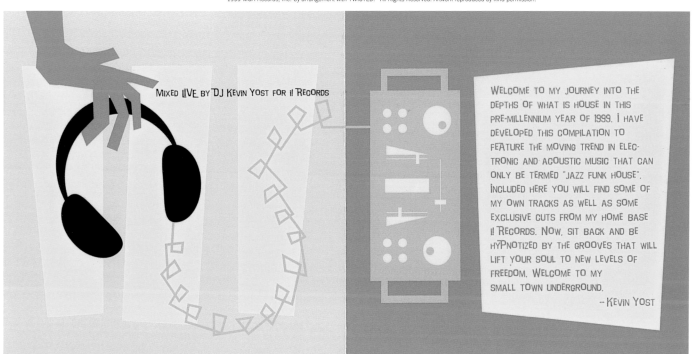

MIXED LIVE BY DJ KEVIN YOST FOR i! RECORDS

WELCOME TO MY JOURNEY INTO THE DEPTHS OF WHAT IS HOUSE IN THIS PRE-MILLENNIUM YEAR OF 1999. I HAVE DEVELOPED THIS COMPILATION TO FEATURE THE MOVING TREND IN ELEC-TRONIC AND ACOUSTIC MUSIC THAT CAN ONLY BE TERMED "JAZZ FUNK HOUSE". INCLUDED HERE YOU WILL FIND SOME OF MY OWN TRACKS AS WELL AS SOME EXCLUSIVE CUTS FROM MY HOME BASE i! RECORDS. NOW, SIT BACK AND BE HYPNOTIZED BY THE GROOVES THAT WILL LIFT YOUR SOUL TO NEW LEVELS OF FREEDOM. WELCOME TO MY SMALL TOWN UNDERGROUND.

-- KEVIN YOST

booklet

KEVIN YOST SMALL TOWN UNDERGROUND *V.A.*

TWISTED America Records 1999 USA TWD-11949
CD, AD, D: STEVEN NEWMAN   D, I: ROB HUDAK   DF: COMPRESSION STUDIOS

アフロ・ブルー AFRO BLUE
井出 靖 YASUSHI IDE
WARNER MUSIC JAPAN 1999 JAPAN WPC6-10015
AD, D: 角田 純一 JUNICHI TSUNODA   AD: 井出 靖 YASUSHI IDE   D: 吉池 康二 KOJI YOSHIIKE
I: 宮永 りさ RISA MIYANAGA   DF: ㈲マナス MANAS INC.

ブラック・ヴェルヴェット BLACK VELVET
井出 靖 YASUSHI IDE
WARNER MUSIC JAPAN 1999 JAPAN WPC6-10014
AD, D: 角田 純一 JUNICHI TSUNODA   AD: 井出 靖 YASUSHI IDE   D: 吉池 康二 KOJI YOSHIIKE
I: 宮永 りさ RISA MIYANAGA   DF: ㈲マナス MANAS INC.

ONE & ONE / REMIX *ROBERT MILES*

MOTOR MUSIC 1996 GERMANY 573 305-2
AD, D, I: EIKE KOENIG I: DIANA PREYER
DF: EIKES GRAFISCHER HORT

WE GOT THE FUNK *POSITIVE FORCE*

SEQUEL RECORDS 1999 UK NEMCD407

THE FRESH FLAVAS OF TOTALLY WIRED *V.A.*

PONY CANYON (ACID JAZZ) 1998 JAPAN PCCY01316
D: 大久 達朗 TATSURO OHISA

JUNGLIST VOL. 2 *V.A.*

avex trax 1997 JAPAN AVCD-11573
AD, D, I: 角田 純一 JUNICHI TSUNODA
D: 田中 純子 JUNKO TANAKA
LOGO DESIGN: 五木田 智央 TOMOO GOKITA
DF: ㈲マナス MANAS INC.

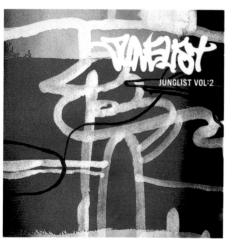

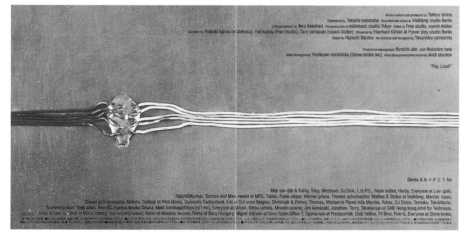

booklet

front

BERLIN TRAX *TAKKYU ISHINO*

Ki/oon RECORDS 1998 JAPAN KSC2213

GLEN SCOTT
WITHOUT VERTIGO

ESCA 7435

epic
ⓟⓒ 1999 Sony Music
Entertainment Inc.
Manufactured by Sony Music
Entertainment (Japan) Inc.
is a Trademark of Sony
Music Entertainment Inc.
(yp)/WARNING: All Rights
Reserved. Unauthorized
duplication is a violation of
applicable laws./STEREO

WITHOUT VERTIGO *GLEN SCOTT*
EPIC RECORDS 1999 JAPAN ESCA7435

WHITEY FORD SINGS THE BLUES *EVERLAST*
TOMMY BOY MUSIC 1998 USA TBCD1236

front   booklet

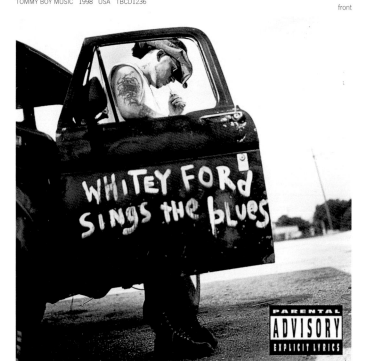

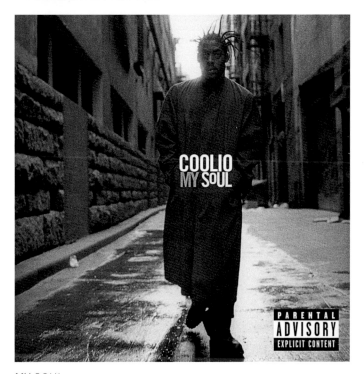

MY SOUL *COOLIO*
TOMMY BOY MUSIC 1997 USA TBCD1180

NEWTONE *NEWTONE*
UNIVERSAL MUSIC 1996 SWEDEN UMD87123

23AM   *ROBERT MILES*
BMG FUNHOUSE 1998 JAPAN BVCP6093

FREEDOM
ROBERT MILES FEARTURING KATHY SLEDGE
BMG FUNHOUSE 1998 JAPAN BVCP8895

BON VOYAGE *UNITED FUTURE ORGANIZATION*

MERCURY 1999 JAPAN PHCR-88
AD, P: 信藤 三雄 MITSUO SHINDO   D: 北澤 剛志 TAKESHI KITAZAWA
P: 石井 文仁 FUMIHITO ISHII   DF: コンテムポラリー・プロダクション CONTEMPORARY PRODUCTION

INSIDE OF YOU *AARON HALL*

MCA RECORDS 1998 USA MVCE-24109

www.the-raft.com/skunk

POST ORGASMIC CHILL *SKUNK ANANSIE*

VIRGIN RECORDS 1999 UK CDVX2881 7243 8 47104 2 2

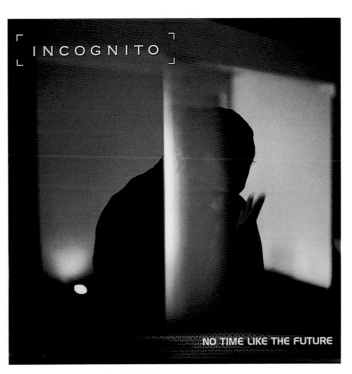

NO TIME LIKE THE FUTURE *INCOGNITO*

MERCURY 1999 UK PHCW1020

front

fold-out booklet

FANMAIL *TLC*
BMG FUNHOUSE 1999 JAPAN BVCA21011

SECOND NATURE *LINDA LEWIS*
SME RECORDS 1995 JAPAN SRCS7754

METAPHOR *DEDE*
EPIC RECORDS 1999 JAPAN ESCA7465

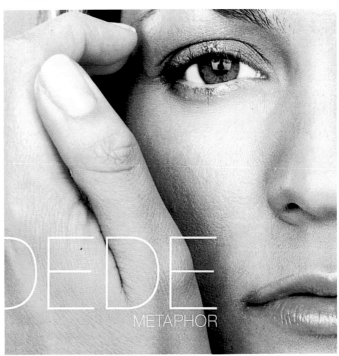

PREMIUMIX *MONDAY MICHIRU*
POLYDOR 1999 JAPAN POCH1779
AD: 信藤 三雄 MITSUO SHINDO D: 新家 敏之 TOSHIYUKI SHINKE P: ナカ NAKA
DF: コンテムポラリー・プロダクション CONTEMPORARY PRODUCTION

THIS IS NOT A LOVE SONG *OMAR*
BMG FUNHOUSE 1997 JAPAN BVCP6059

STILL IN THE GAME *KEITH SWEAT*
ELEKTRA 1998 USA 7559-62262-2

Album artwork used courtesy of Elektra Entertainment Group Inc.

SOUL HOUSE   *V.A.*

NIPPON CROWN   1998   JAPAN   CRCF2031
D: TRANS TRUMP

PLAYER'S CALL   *ORAN JUICE JONES FEAT. STU LARGE*

TOMMY BOY MUSIC   1997   USA   TBCD1179

TIME CAPSULE   *IZIT*

quattro label   1998   JAPAN   QTCY2123/2124

ONE DAY IT'LL ALL MAKE SENSE   *COMMON*

SME RECORDS   1997   JAPAN   SRCS8256

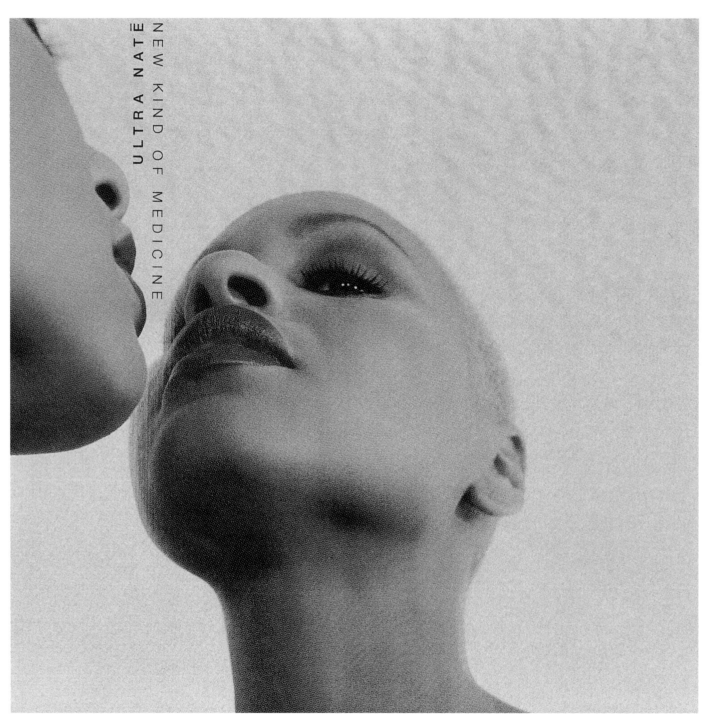

ULTRA NATĒ

NEW KIND OF MEDICINE

NEW KIND OF MEDICINE *ULTRA NATĒ*
STRICTLY RHYTHM RECORDS 1998 USA SR12555

SITUATION: CRITICAL   *ULTRA NATĒ*

cutting edge   1998   JAPAN   CTCR13106

RESURRECTION   *FESTIVAL*

DISKO B   1998   GERMANY   DB67CD
CD, AD, D, P, I, DF: STRADA

JESSICA   *JESSICA*

avex trax   1998   JAPAN   AVCZ95111

NEW LIFE   *RUFFNECK FEATURING YAVAHN*

cutting edge   1999   JAPAN   CTCR13116

SUPERNATURAL   *DES'REE*

EPIC RECORDS   1998   JAPAN   ESCA7333

THE TOUR   *MARY J. BLIGE*
MCA RECORDS 1998 USA MCAD-11848

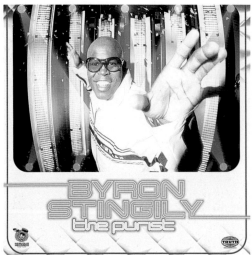

LA VIE EN LILALI   *KIM'KAY*
EMI MUSIC BELGIUM 1998 BELGIUM 7243 4986982 0
CD, AD, D, I: SVEN MASTBOOMS P: PHILIP MATTHYS
I: JEROEN VAN OMME DF: SEVEN PRODUCTIONS

THE PURIST   *BYRON STINGILY*
cutting edge 1998 JAPAN CTCR14084

T.T.Y.F.（TRIP TILL YOU FLIP） *DJ MD*

CNR MUSIC 1997 BELGIUM 2102273
CD, AD, D, I: SVEN MASTBOOMS P: ROGER DICKMANS I: JEROEN VAN OMME DF: SEVEN PRODUCTIONS

I AM... *NAS*

SME RECORDS 1999 JAPAN SRCS8777

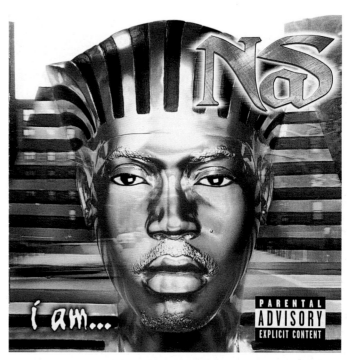

Album artwork used courtesy of Elektra Entertainment Group Inc.

SCOUTS HONOR...BY WAY OF BLOOD *RAMPAGE*

ELEKTRA 1997 USA 62022-2

ORDER IN THE COURT *QUEEN LATIFAH*

MOTOWN RECORD 1998 USA 536 906-2

HELLO NASTY *BEASTIE BOYS*

CAPITOL RECORDS 1998 USA 7243 4 95723 2 4

front

back

1 Super Disco Breakin'
2 The Move
3 Remote Control
4 Song for the Man
5 Just a Test
6 Body Movin' ◦
7 Intergalactic
8 Sneakin' Out the Hospital
9 Putting Shame in Your Game
10 Flowin' Prose
11 And Me
12 Three MC's and One DJ
13 Can't, Won't, Don't Stop ◦
14 Song for Junior ◦
15 I Don't Know
16 The Negotiation Limerick File ◦
17 Electrify #
18 Picture This #
19 Unite
20 Dedication ▸
21 Dr. Lee, PhD ◦
22 Instant Death

GUY ORNADEL ♛ LICENSED TO THRILL

PLAYER ONE GET READY

18 STEVE MORLEY *REINCARNATIONS*
DJ JamX and De Leon's OutMonde Remix
Written and Produced M. Allol
Licensed from BPM Dance, NL.
Published by Les Editions Apocalypse.
℗1999 Neo Records Ltd.

11 PARKER AND AND KLEIN *GENERATOR*
Power Club Mix
Written and produced by Stephen Parker
and Stephane Pezlov. Published by BMG
Universal Music Publishing.
℗1999 Bonzai Music.

12 CRAZY MALAMUTE *FREE TO RIDE*
Written and Produced by ???????
?????????
?????????

back

front

LICENCED TO THRILL *GUY ORNADEL*

AUTOMATIC RECORDS 1999 UK AUT0604CD
CD, AD, D: RIAN HUGHES P: JOHN R. WARD DF: DEVICE

DEEPER CONCENTRATION   *V.A.*

UNITED GRUVS 1999 JAPAN MKCA-1005
D: GATHRIE DOLIN (BRAND A)   PAINTING BY: DOZE

LOVE THE LIVE   ACID JAZZ LIVE   *V.A.*

PONY CANYON (ACID JAZZ) 1998 JAPAN PCCY-01315
D: 松村 麻有美 MAYUMI MATSUMURA

A PRINCE AMONG THIEVES   *PRINCE PAUL*

TOMMY BOY MUSIC 1999 USA TBCD1210

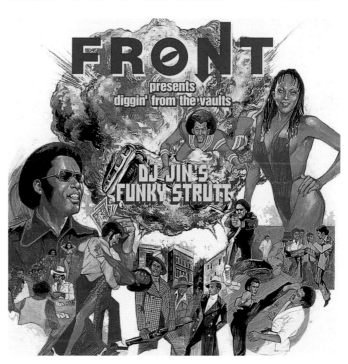

DJ JIN'S FUNKY STRUTT   *V.A.*

VICTOR ENTERTAINMENT 1998 JAPAN VICP60196

AUTOMATIC ANTHEMS-NEW BRITISH HOUSE *V.A.*
AUTOMATIC RECORDS 1997 UK AUTO601CD
CD, AD, D, I: RIAN HUGHES DF: DEVICE

back   front

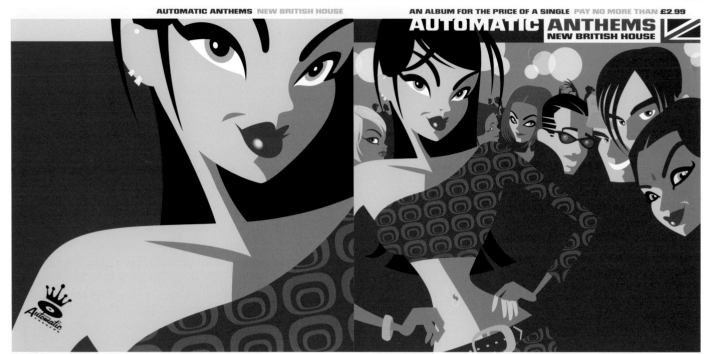

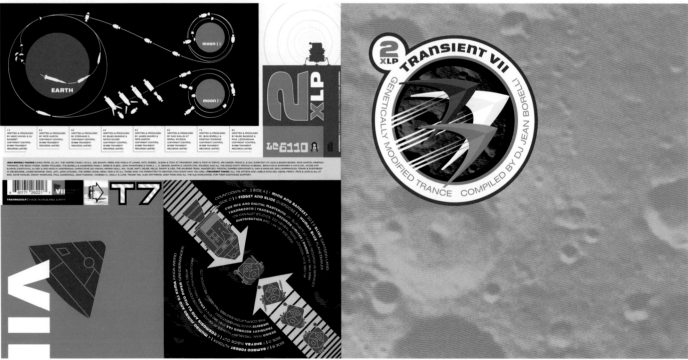

back   front

TRANSIENT 7 *V.A.*
TRANSIENT RECORDS 1999 UK TRANR622LP
CD, AD, D, I: RIAN HUGHES DF: DEVICE

UNSEQUENCED *ACID JUNKIES*

DJAX RECORDS 1996 THE NETHERLANDS DJAX-UP-CD14
CD, AD, D: J.J.F.G. BORRENBERGS DF: STOERE BINKEN DESIGN

LASS DIE SONNE REIN
DIE FANTASTISCHEN VIER

SONY MUSIC ENTERTAINMENT (GERMANY)
1993 GERMANY 12-659232-19
CD: OLIVER-A KRIMMEL, ANJA OSTERWALDER DF: I_D BÜRO

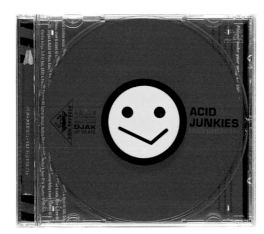

LET'S GO TO THE PARTY
POCO LOCO GANG

BIT MUSIC / CNR MUSIC 1999 BELGIUM ARC309
CD, AD, D, I: SVEN MASTBOOMS DF: SEVEN PRODUCTIONS

POCO LOCO *POCO LOCO GANG*

BIT MUSIC / CNR MUSIC 1998 BELGIUM ARC309
CD, AD, D, I: SVEN MASTBOOMS DF: SEVEN PRODUCTIONS

GET UP (THE SEQUEL)
TECHNOTRONIC

ARS PRODUCTIONS 1997 BELGIUM 740198-3
CD, AD, D, I: SVEN MASTBOOMS DF: SEVEN PRODUCTIONS

WHY? *TASHA*

SONY MUSIC ENTERTAINMENT (BELGIUM)
1996 BELGIUM 28-663003-14
CD, AD, D, I: SVEN MASTBOOMS DF: SEVEN PRODUCTIONS

CLASSIC HIP HOP 2 *V.A.*
BEECHWOOD MUSIC 1996 UK CUTSCD35

CLASSIC G-FUNK *V.A.*
BEECHWOOD MUSIC 1997 UK CUTSCD39

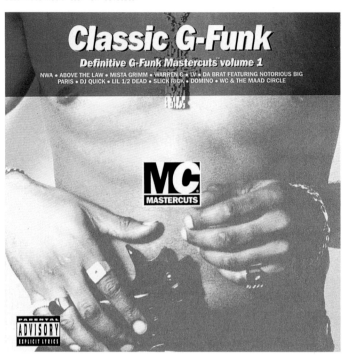

GREATEST TITS *E-ROTIC*
INTERCORD 1998 GERMANY BLOW UP INT8 22620 2
CD: OLIVER-A KRIMMEL, ANJA OSTERWALDER I: ZORAN DF: I_D BÜRO

INSPIRATION *JAM PACK*
TOSHIBA EMI 1999 JAPAN TOCP65176

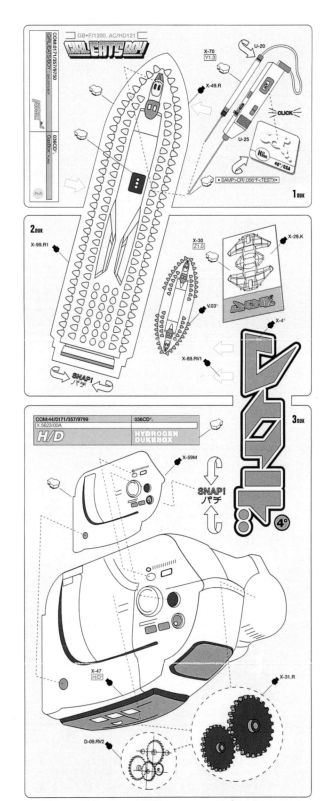

THRILLED BY VELOCITY & DISTORTION *GIRL EATS BOY*
HYDROGEN DUKEBOX 1998 UK DUKE036CD
DF: YACHT ASSOCIATES

front

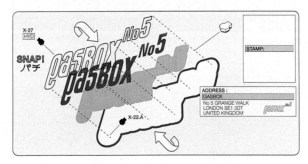

booklet

front

THE THREE E.P.'S *THE BETA BAND*
TOSHIBA EMI 1998 JAPAN TOCP-50655

disk

front

back

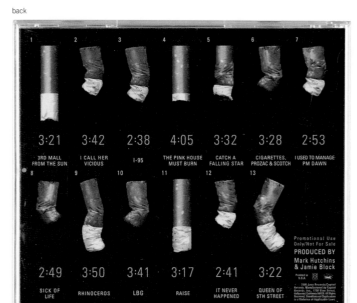

inner

TIMING IS EVERYTHING *BLOCK*

CAPITOL RECORDS 1998 USA DPRO7087 6 12893 2 9
CD, AD: STEFAN SAGMEISTER D: HJALTI KARLSSON P: SUSAN STOVA I: BARBARA EHRBAR CW: JAMIE BLOCK DF: SAGMEISTER INC.

UP UP UP UP UP UP   *ANI DIFRANCO*
P-VINE NonStop / BMG   1999   JAPAN   PVCP-8744

MAG EARWHIG!   *GUIDED BY VOICES*
MATADOR RECORDS   1997   USA   OLE241-2
D: BOB OHE & MARK OHE (A BURNING LIZARD CREATION)

PONYOAK   *KLEEN EX-GIRL WONDER*
MARCH RECORDS / ROCK RECORDS (JAPAN)   1999   JAPAN   RCCY1038

DOSE   *LATIN PLAYBOYS*
ATLANTIC   1999   USA   7567-83173-2

LIVE IN N.Y.C '78   *TODD RUNDGREN*
NIPPON CROWN   1999   JAPAN   CRCL-7701
D: 井上 幹也 MIKIYA INOUE

front

booklet

さくら SAKURA *SOUTHERN ALL STARS*
VICTOR ENTERTAINMENT / TAISHITA 1998 JAPAN VICL60300

WINTER BIRDS *SEELY*

TWENTY14.COM 1999 USA T14GH004
CD, AD, D, I, DF: GRAPHIC HAVOC AVISUALAGENCY P: ALEX WHITE

back   front

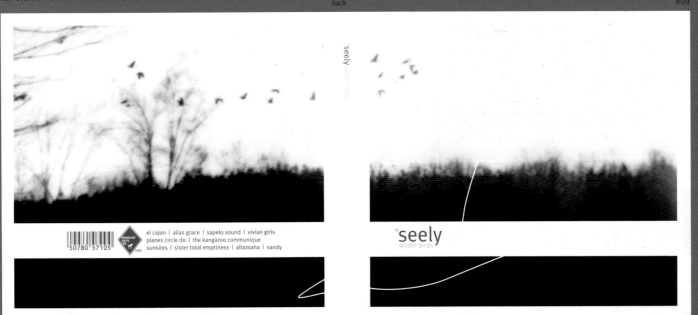

SHADOW *KARAFUTO*

Ki/oon RECORDS 1998 JAPAN KSC2235

蛍 HOTARU *b-flower*

TOSHIBA EMI 1997 JAPAN TOCT4090
AD, D: 坂村 健次 KENJI SAKAMURA P: 外山 繁 SHIGERU TOYAMA
DF: コロムビア・クリエイティヴ COLUMBIA CREATIVE INC.

REVOLT *3 COLORS RED*

EPIC RECORDS 1999 JAPAN ESCA7442

HAWAII   *THE HIGH LLAMAS*
V2 MUSIC 1998 UK V2CI0010
I: KEV HOPPEN   ART DIRECTION: M2 AND SEAN O'HAGAN   DESIGN BY M2

ORANGE CRATE ART
BRIAN WILSON AND VAN DYKE PARKS
WARNER BROS. RECORDS 1995 USA 9362-45427-2

COLD AND BOUNCY   *THE HIGH LLAMAS*
V2 MUSIC   1998   UK   V2CI0007
I: KEV HOPPEN   ART DIRECTION: M2 AND SEAN O'HAGAN   DESIGN BY M2

POISONOUS LIFE   *I'M BEING GOOD*
INFINITE CHUG   1999   UK   CHUG12
D: ANDREW CLARE

BOOKSHELF ADVENTURES   *JUMPROPE*
FLAVOUR OF SOUND   1998   JAPAN   TFCK-87605

THE GREAT NOSTALGIA·DRIVE   *CARNATION*
COLUMBIA   1996   JAPAN   CODA921
AD, D: 坂村 健次 KENJI SAKAMURA
DF: コロムビア・クリエイティヴ COLUMBIA CREATIVE INC.

ジョーイ JOEY   ボイド *VOID*
MIDI   1999   JAPAN   MDCL1344

DOPAMINE *MITCHELL FROOM*
EAST WEST JAPAN 1998 JAPAN AMCY-2773

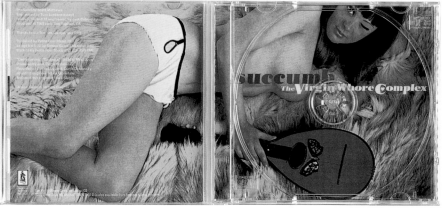

front

inner without disk

SUCCUMB *THE VIRGIN-WHORE COMPLEX*
EMPEROR NORTON RECORDS / ROCK RECORDS (JAPAN) 1998 JAPAN
RCCY-1020

SIMPLY FABOO   *THE GENTLE PEOPLE*
FLAVOUR OF SOUND 1999 JAPAN TFCK-87620
P: ANTON WATTS   SLEEVE BY KAORU AT NARC   OUTFITS: ROJA VON GALAXY
HAIR: RAPHAEL SALLEY   MAKE-UP: TANYA CHIANALE

MIX GENTLY   *THE GENTLE PEOPLE*
FLAVOUR OF SOUND 1997 JAPAN TFCK-87571
D: JOHNNY CLAYTON

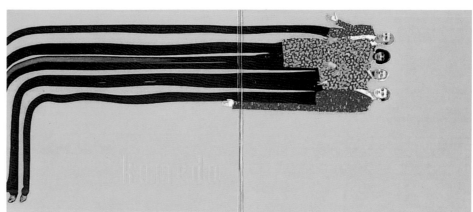

fold-out package

WHAT MAKES IT GO?   *KOMEDA*
N.O.N.S. RECORDS / ROCK RECORDS (JAPAN)
1998 JAPAN RCCY1009

コメダマニア POP PÅ SVENSKA   *KOMEDA*
PIONEER LDC (NORTH OF NO SOUTH RECORDS) 1993 JAPAN PICP1136

WITHOUT ONION *GREAT3*
TOSHIBA EMI 1998 JAPAN TOCT-10414
D: 打越 俊明 TOSHIAKI UCHIKOSHI (KING CAY LAB)

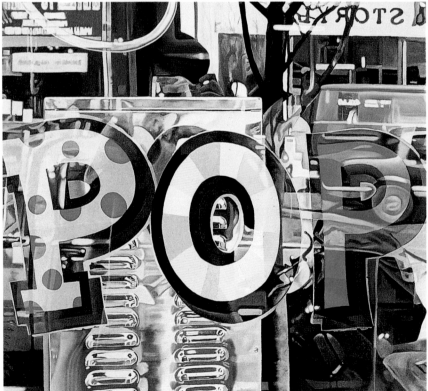

CARNIVAL BOY *TOBIN SPROUT*
MATADOR RECORDS 1996 USA OLE216-2
D: TOBIN SPROUT

THE KINDNESS OF STRANGERS *SPOCK'S BEARD*

VICTOR ENTERTAINMENT 1998 JAPAN VICP60234

MOVING CAREFUL *HAYDEN*

ONLY HEARTS 1997 JAPAN OHCY-5

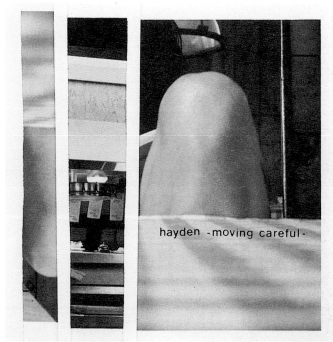

ツカレタカオデコンニチハ TSUKARETA KAODE KONNICHIWA
SUPER TRAPP

BMG FUNHOUSE 1997 JAPAN BVCR-784
AD, D, DF: ㈲サイレントグラフィックス SILENT GRAPHICS, INC.

BLACK FOLIAGE *THE OLIVIA TREMOR CONTROL*

FLYDADDY 1999 UK V2CL35
ARTIST: W. CULLEN HART LAYOUT: W. CULLEN HART, BILL DOSS, CHRIS BILLHEIMER

SAM PREKOP *SAM PREKOP*
THRILL JOCKEY 1999 USA THRILL061

LEGEND OF THE BLOOD YETI *THE THIRTEEN GHOSTS*

INFINITE CHUG 1997 UK CHUG5CD
D: ANDREW CLARE

KEEP CALM AND DIG *SMALL THINGS*

INFINITE CHUG 1998 UK CHUG8
D: ANDREW CLARE

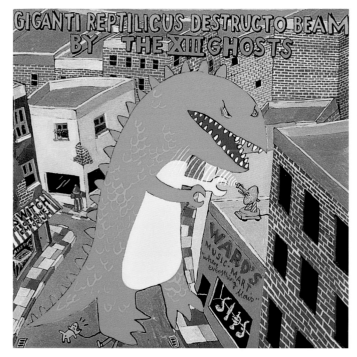

GIGANTI REPTILICUS DESTRUCTO BEAM *THE THIRTEEN GHOSTS*

SCATTER 1995 UK SCATTER04CD
D: ANDREW CLARE

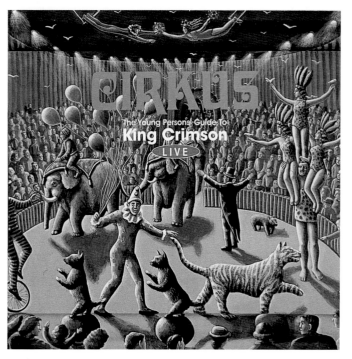

CIRKUS *KING CRIMSON*

PONY CANYON (DISCIPLINE GLOBAL MOBILE) 1999 JAPAN
PCCY01356

HEAVEN   *JAYWALK*
MELDAC CORPORATION 1999 JAPAN MECR-30120
DF: スントー事務所 SUNTO OFFICE

THE FORCE   *T.M.REVOLUTION*
ANTINOS RECORDS 1999 JAPAN ARCJ91

13　*BLUR*
TOSHIBA EMI 1999 JAPAN TOCP-65091

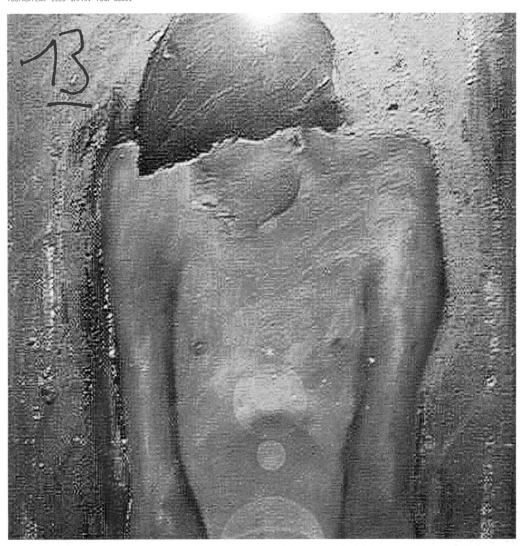

1999 REMIX SINGLE（PROPOSAL）　*V.A.*

99.3 THE FOX 1998 CANADA 993-99
D: TROY BAILLY, STEPHEN PARKES, DAVID PAPINEAU　DF: PROTOTYPE DESIGN

MOTHER　大高ジャッキー *OHTAKA JACKY*

ONLY HEARTS 1999 JAPAN OHCA-22
I: 村松 剛 TAKESHI MURAMATSU

front

back

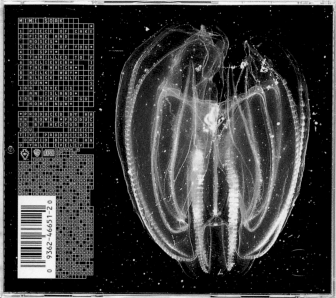

inner

SOAR *MIMI*

LUAKA BOP   1998   USA   9 46651-2
CD, AD: STEFAN SAGMEISTER   D: HJALTI KARLSSON
P: JOSEPH COLTICE, CARL MAY, STOCK   CW: MIMI GOESE   DF: SAGMEISTER INC.

PAXTON

WHICH WAY DO YOU GO?
I'M NOT LIKE EVERYBODY ELSE
SO INTO YOU
JOHN & JOE
THE MORNING SONG
FATHERLESS SONS
I WANT YOU NOW!
NUMBER ONE

ALL IN THE PAST
HUH?
FALLING BEHIND
SLAMMED

7 93018 28322 9

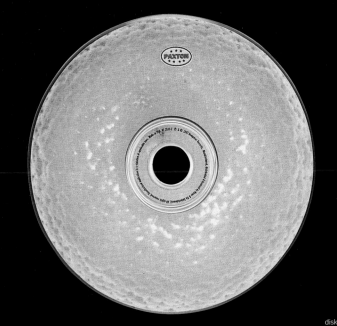

PAXTON *PAXTON*

NEMPEROR RECORDS 1997 USA RT2832-2
CD, AD, I: STEFAN SAGMEISTER D: HJALTI KARLSSON P: NEAL PRESTON, DARRYL SNAYCHOR, TOM SCHIERLITZ
I: HJALTI KARLSSON CW: PAXTON DF: SAGMEISTER INC.

front

back

inner without disk

MODERN IST WIEDER IN *EISEN*

DYNAMO MUSIC 1998 GERMANY DYNAMO980201
CD, AD, D: LAURENZ BICK P: PHILIP LETHEN DF: VS.42 DESIGNSTUDIO

front

back

sleeve back

I WASN'T BUILT TO GET UP   *THE SUPERNATURALS*

PARLOPHONE RECORDS   1998   UK   7243 8 85724 2 2

front

booklet

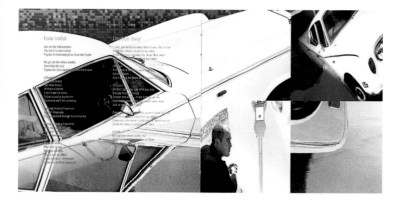

disk

BE HERE NOW *OASIS*
EPIC RECORDS 1997 JAPAN ESCA6767

100% COTTON   *SUPER TRAPP*

BMG FUNHOUSE   1999   JAPAN   BVCS-21008 (74321-164776-2)
AD, D, DF: ㈲サイレントグラフィックス SILENT GRAPHICS, INC.
P: 蜷川 実花 MIKA NINAGAWA

SUPER TRAPP

PLANET 25：30   *SUPER TRAPP*

BMG FUNHOUSE   1999   JAPAN   BVCS-29009 (74321-66487-2)
AD, D, DF: ㈲サイレントグラフィックス SILENT GRAPHICS, INC.
P: 蜷川 実花 MIKA NINAGAWA

*SUPER TRAPP
'Wuthering' being a significant provincial adjective, descriptive of the
atmospheric tumult to which its station is exposed in stormy weather.
Pure, bracing ventilation they must have up there at all times.

FIN DE SIÈCLE *THE DIVINE COMEDY*
SETANTA RECORDS 1998 UK V2CI0005
AD, D: ROB CRANE   P: KEVIN LIESTENBERG   DF: SATTELITE (LONDON)

NO ONE IS REALLY BEAUTIFUL   *JUDE*

MAVERICK RECORDING COMPANY   1998   USA   9 47087-2

jewel case with disk

ACE A'S + KILLER B'S *DODGY*
MERCURY 1998 UK PHCR1654

BUTTER 08 *BUTTER 08*
GRAND ROYAL 1996 USA GR029
CD: FRITZ MICHAUD AD, D: MIKE MILLS P: JOE WITTKOP DF: DIVERSIFIED

NOSTALGIE *NAVIGATOR*
SWARF FINGER RECORDS 1998 UK SF032

front without case

月面讃歌 ANTHEM OF THE MOON *MOONRIDERS*
Ki/oon RECORDS 1998 JAPAN KSC2230
AD, D: 加藤 靖隆 YASUTAKA KATO P: 地主 晋 SHIN JINUSHI

THE BLUES SCENE *V.A.*

THE DECCA RECORD COMPANY 1999 UK 844 801-2
PACKAGE DESIGNER: PHIL SMEE AT WALDOS DESIGN AND DREAM EMPORIUM COMPILATION: BRIAN HOGG

THE ROCK 'N' ROLL SCENE *V.A.*

THE DECCA RECORD COMPANY 1999 UK 844 892-2
PACKAGE DESIGNER: PHIL SMEE AT WALDOS DESIGN AND DREAM EMPORIUM
SLEEVE NOTES BY DEKE WHEELER AND JOHN REED COMPILATION: DEKE WHEELER

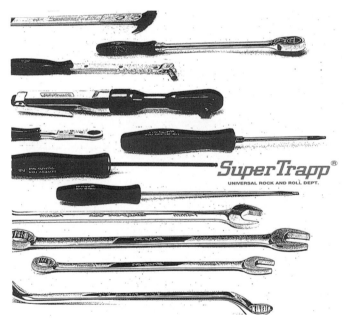

ポイント POINT *SUPER TRAPP*

BMG FUNHOUSE 1997 JAPAN BVCR-8811 (74321-51860-2)
AD, D, DF: ㈲サイレントグラフィックス SILENT GRAPHICS, INC.

MASTERTAPE *MEGAPEARLS*

1999 GERMANY
CD: OLIVER-A KRIMMEL, ANJA OSTERWALDER D: FRANK ZUBER P: I_D TEAM DF: I_D BÜRO

WALKING IN THE RHYTHM *FISHMANS*
POLYDOR 1997 JAPAN POCH-1653

front

fold-out booklet

rock pop ⓑ

MIRACLE OF SCIENCE *MARSHALL CRENSHAW*

RAZOR & TIE ENTERTAINMENT 1997 USA RT2823-2
CD, AD: STEFAN SAGMEISTER D: VERONICA OH P: TOM SCHIERLITZ
CW: MARSHALL CRENSHAW DF: SAGMEISTER INC.

front

back

jewel case with disk

booklet

赤いタンバリン RED TAMBOURINE
BLANKEY JET CITY

POLYDOR 1998 JAPAN POCH1673
AD: 信藤 三雄 MITSUO SHINDO D: 大箭 亮二 RYOJI OHYA P: ナカ NAKA
DF: コンテムポラリー・プロダクション CONTEMPORARY PRODUCTION

1   2   3

front

THE IMPOSSIBLE SHUFFLE *CLOUDBERRY JAM*
quattro label 1997 JAPAN QTCY-2105

back

WHAT ANOTHER MAN SPILLS *LAMBCHOP*

MERGE RECORDS 1998 USA MRG146CD

front

back

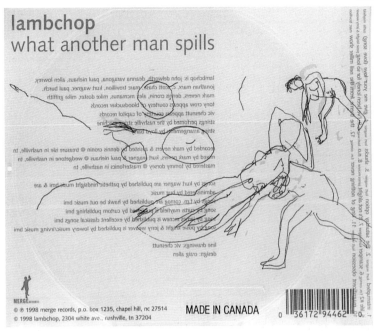

AN EASTERN WESTERN COLLECTED WORKS
DAVID SHEA

SUB ROSA 1998 GERMANY SR134
ART COVER: DOMINIQUE GOBLET

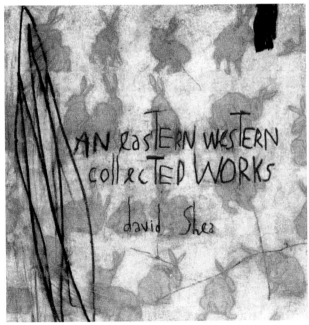

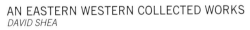

front

back

front

sleeve front

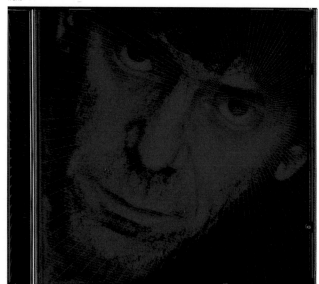

inner

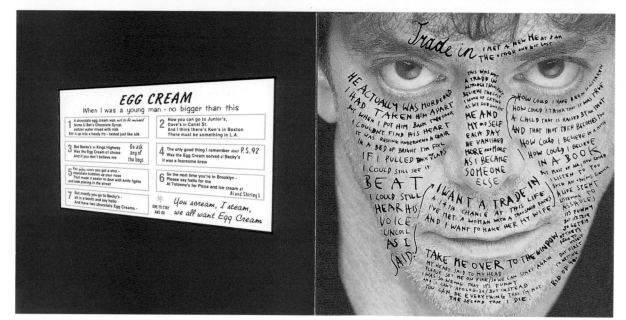

booklet

SET THE TWILIGHT REELING *LOU REED*

WARNER BORS. RECORDS 1997 USA 9 46159-2
CD, AD: STEFAN SAGMEISTER D: VERONICA OH P: TIMOTHY GREENFIELD SANDERS
I: TONY FITZPATRICK CW: LOU REED DF: SAGMEISTER INC.

front

sleeve front

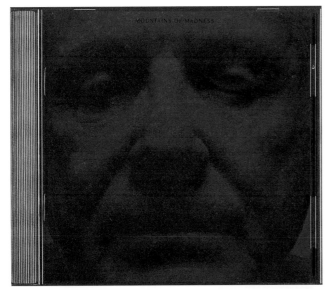

inner

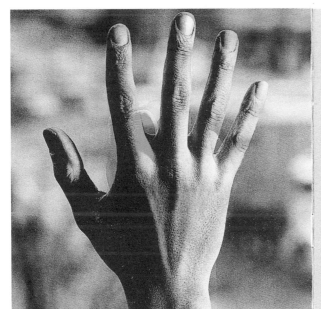

All songs written by hp   ©zinkopated music (ASCAP)

Arranged by   H a n s P l a t z g u m e r   guitars, vocals, gimmicks
D a v i d Wasik drums & percussion U v e y Batruel   bass

Except for track 5: lyrics by hp lovecraft. Used by kind permission of Arkham House Publishers, Inc.
and track 14: written & performed by ub. Track 15 taken from the soundtrack to the motion picture 'Tief Oben'
('Deep Up There'). Courtesy of Extrafilm/Vienna.

Recorded at Soundgarden, Hamburg

Christian Mevs & Chris von Rautenkranz   Christian Mevs & hp
Engineered by   Mixed by

Tracks 2 and 4 recorded and mixed at Baby Monster, NYC. Engineered by Steve Burgh and Andy
Ryder. Tracks 5, 10, 11 and 15 recorded and mixed at AnTon, Austria. Engineered by Charly Petermichl and
Klaus Anton Bichler.

hp & z.   Mastered by Howie Weinberg at Master Disk, NYC.
Produced by
Dedicated to Phil Lynott (1951 - 1986).

A&R, merchandise: Charles A. Caronia & Rob Grant
Energy Records 545 8th Ave 17th floor NY, NY 10018 fax: (212) 695-5584

Sagmeister Inc. (212) 647-1789   Tom Schierlitz
Art Designed by   Photography by

Contact: Thomas Radovan   Vorachstr. 65
A - 6890 Lustenau ph/fax: (43) 5577-89663
Zinker Europe
p. o. box 1619 NY, NY 10009
Zinker U.S.

Appreciation											
Trevor Peres Gaga Klocker	Charley PM the Ballets	Matt Hanks Rich Johnson	Eric Lemasters Michelle Wakefield	Sana B. Bobs	Michi Danner Thomas & Lucy	Peter Batruel & everybody else at Batruels	Kai Fricka Gregory Sammons	Hannes Baumann Geco & Zutty	Sven the whole Wasik crew	Vic Firth sticks Paiste cymbals Int.	DW drums Folks at Energy

PLAY IT LOUD! YES, PLAY IT VERY VERY LOUD!!

booklet

MOUNTAINS OF MADNESS   *H.P.ZINKER*

ENERGY RECORDS 1997 USA NRG81113-2
CD, AD: STEFAN SAGMEISTER D: VERONICA OH P: TOM SCHIERLITZ
CW: HANS PLATZGUMMER DF: SAGMEISTER INC.

front

jewel case with disk

booklet

NINE LIVES *AEROSMITH*

COLUMBIA RECORDS 1997 USA CK67547
CD, AD: STEFAN SAGMEISTER D: HJALTI KARLSSON P: SCOTT SCHAFER
I: HUNGRY DOG STUDIOS DF: SAGMEISTER INC.

front

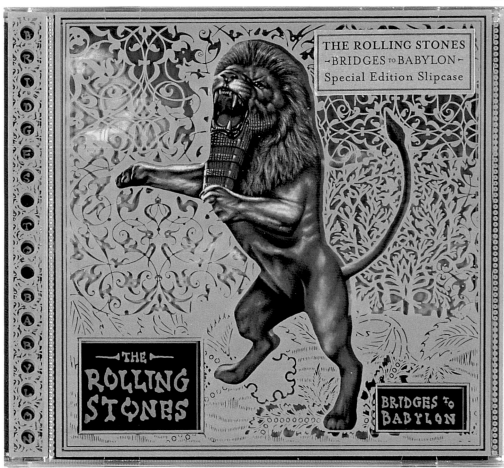

www.the-rolling-stones.com

inner

BRIDGES TO BABYLON   *THE ROLLING STONES*

VIRGIN RECORDS / PROMOTONE B.V.   1997   UK   INAV7243-8-44712-2-4
CD, AD: STEFAN SAGMEISTER   D: HJALTI KARLSSON   P: MAX VADUKUL
I: KEVIN MURPHY, GERARD HOWLAND, ALAN AYERS   CW: JAGGER, RICHARDS   DF: SAGMEISTER INC.

front

LOW POWERS   *HAJIME TACHIBANA & LOW POWERS*
FOR LIFE   1997   JAPAN   FLCF-3701
AD: 立花 ハジメ HAJIME TACHIBANA
D: 千原 航 KOH CHIHARA   P: 井上 よういち YOUICHI INOUE
DF: 立花ハジメデザイン HAJIME TACHIBANA DESIGN

disk

BLENDER *THE MURMURS*
MCA RECORDS 1998 USA MCAD-11802   front

jewel case with disk

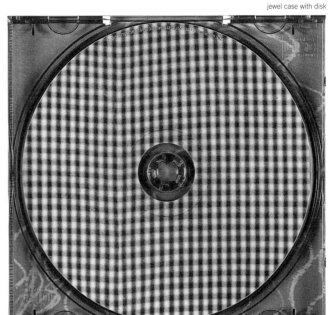

DOSAGE *COLLECTIVE SOUL*
ATLANTIC 1999 USA 83162-2

SHAKE IT *THE RAGING MEN*
SILVERTONE RECORDS 1998 THE NETHERLANDS 0518292
AD, D: ERIK KESSELS P: ANDRÉ THIJSSEN CW: JOHAN KRAMER DF: KESSELSKRAMER

OPEN ALL NIGHT *MARC ALMOND*
BLUE STAR RECORDS 1999 UK BSRCD001

変身 HENSHIN *ORIGINAL LOVE*
PONY CANYON 1999 JAPAN PCCA-01288
AD: 駿東 宏 HIROSHI SUNTO DF: スントー事務所 SUNTO OFFICE

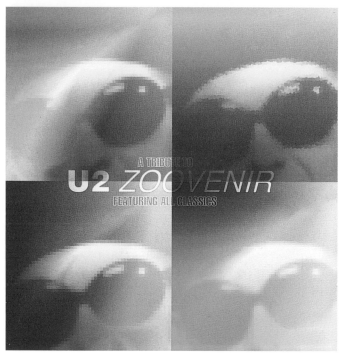

SOUVENIR A TRIBUTE TO U2 FEATURING ALL CLASSICS *V.A.*
TRIBUTE RECORDS 1998 SWEDEN TR025

MOVE ON! *MASAHARU*
PONY CANYON 1997 JAPAN PCCA-01088
AD, D: 三ツ井 正澄 MASAZUMI MITSUI P: 坂崎 恵一 KEIICHI SAKAZAKI DF: ㈱アートワークス ART WORKS INC.

A / COLLECTION   *MATT BIANCO*
VICTOR ENTERTAINMENT   1998   JAPAN   VICP60490
case front

front

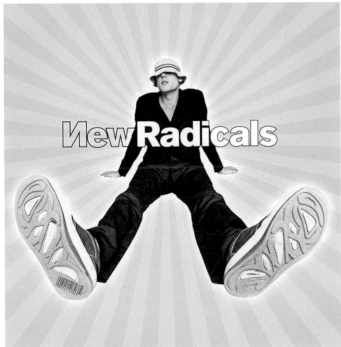

MAYBE YOU'VE BEEN BRAINWASHED TOO.   *NEW RADICALS*
MCA RECORDS   1998   USA   MCAD-11858

THE FRIEND I ONCE HAD   *CLUB 8*
FLAVOUR OF SOUND   1998   JAPAN   TFCK-87596

front

TROPICALIA *BECK*
GEFFEN RECORDS 1998 USA GEFDM-22365
D: BECK HANSEN CD DRAWING: BECK HANSEN LAYOUT: ROBERT FISHER

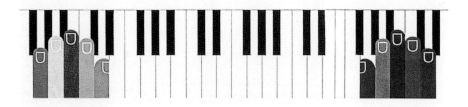

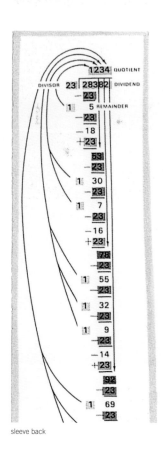

sleeve back

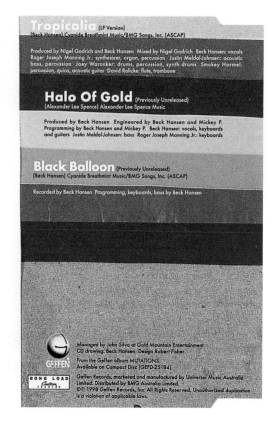

disk

front

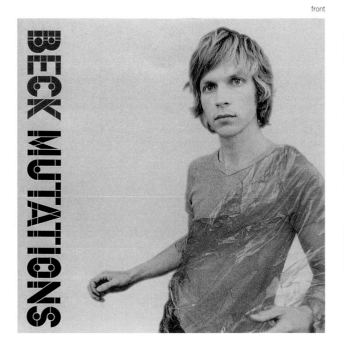

back

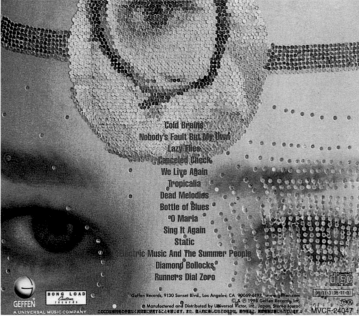

Cold Brains
Nobody's Fault But My Own
Lazy Flies
Canceled Check
We Live Again
Tropicalia
Dead Melodies
Bottle of Blues
O Maria
Sing It Again
Static
Electric Music And The Summer People
Diamond Bollocks
Runners Dial Zero

booklet

MUTATIONS *BECK*

GEFFEN RECORDS 1998 USA GEFDM-25309
AD: TIM HAWKINSON, BECK HANSEN ORIGINAL ARTWORKS: TIM HAWKINSON
ART DESIGNED: ROBERT FISHER COVER PHOTO: CHARLIE GROSS

booklet

rock pop

TITLE

TNT *TORTOISE*
TOKUMA JAPAN COMMUNICATIONS 1998 JAPAN TKCB-71338

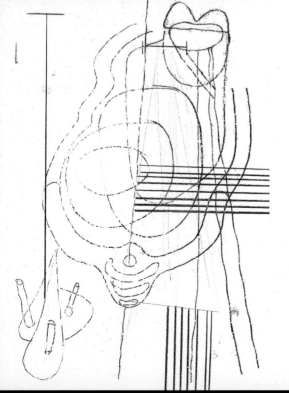

CAMOUFLEUR *GASTR DEL SOL*
DRAG CITY 1998 USA DC133CD

EVE6 *EVE6*
BMG FUNHOUSE 1999 JAPAN BVCP21048

BOOK OF SPELLS *THE BONE SHAKERS*
VIRGIN RECORDS AMERICA 1997 USA VPBCD40 7243 8 42789 2 2

front

inner

SKELETON KEY *SKELETON KEY*
MOTEL RECORDS 1997 USA ROOM2
CD, AD, I: STEFAN SAGMEISTER   D, I: VERONICA OH   I: ERIK SANKO
CW: SKELETON KEY   DF: SAGMEISTER INC.

WONSAPONATIME *JOHN LENNON*

YOKO ONO / CAPITOL RECORDS 1998 USA 7243 4 97639 2 0

front

disk

INTO THE SUN *SEAN LENNON*

TOSHIBA EMI 1998 JAPAN TOCP-50555

HALF HORSE HALF MUSICIAN *SEAN LENNON*

TOSHIBA EMI 1999 JAPAN TOCP61010

シトラス e.p   CITRUS e.p   *ADVANTAGE LUCY*
TOSHIBA EMI 1998 JAPAN TOCT4116
D: セキ ユリヲ YURIO SEKI（ROCKET） I: 高田 里香 RIKA TAKADA

A TUNE A DAY   *THE SUPERNATURALS*
PARLOPHONE RECORDS 1998 UK 7243 4 96066 2 3

HELLO MATE!   *ADVANTAGE LUCY*
TOSHIBA EMI 1998 JAPAN TOCT-4125
D: セキ ユリヲ YURIO SEKI（ROCKET） I: ソリマチ アキラ AKIRA SORIMACHI

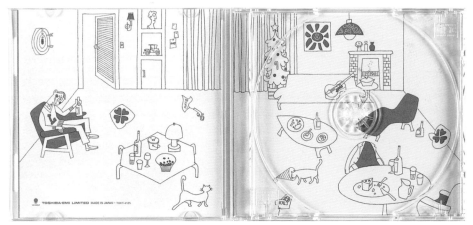

inner without disk

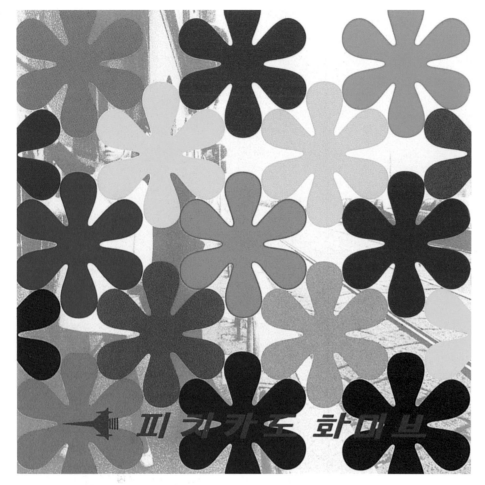

REMIX ALBUM: HAPPY END OF YOU
PIZZICATO FIVE

MATADOR RECORDS 1998 USA OLE282-2
D: KONISHI YASUHARU & MARK OHE

NONSTOP TO TOKYO E.P. *PIZZICATO FIVE*

HEAT WAVE 1999 JAPAN COCA50119
CD: 小西 康陽 YASUHARU KONISHI AD: 信藤 三雄 MITSUO SHINDO
D: 大石 裕子 YUKO OHISHI P: 鶴田 直樹 NAOKI TSURUTA
DF: コンテムポラリー・プロダクション CONTEMPORARY PRODUCTION

4N5 *HI-POSI*

HEAT WAVE 1999 JAPAN COCP-50122
AD, P: 信藤 三雄 MITSUO SHINDO
D: 新家 敏之 TOSHIYUKI SHINKE I: STEPHEN CAMBELL
DF: コンテムポラリー・プロダクション CONTEMPORARY PRODUCTION

ONE THOUSAND 20TH CENTURY CHAIRS   *KAHIMI KARIE*
POLYDOR 1998 JAPAN POCP-7297
D: 北山 雅和 MASAKAZU KITAYAMA

HOWL   *ends*
VICTOR ENTERTAINMENT 1998 JAPAN VICL-60289

front

back

スリル・マーチ THRILL MARCH   朝日 美穂 *MIHO ASAHI*
SONY MUSIC ENTERTAINMENT (JAPAN) 1999 JAPAN AICT-1064
AD, D: 角田 純一 JUNICHI TSUNODA   P: 野口 貴司 TAKASHI NOGUCHI
CW: 五木田 智央 TOMOO GOKITA   DF: ㈲マナス MANAS INC.

うたき UTAKI　小谷 美紗子 MISAKO ODANI
UNIVERSAL VICTOR　1999　JAPAN　MVCH-29030
AD, D: 中村 智 SATOSHI NAKAMURA (SUPER SCARET)　A COPPER PLATE ENGRAVING: 水上 多摩江 TAMAE MIZUKAMI

股旅 MATATABI　　*奥田 民生 OKUDA TAMIO*
SME RECORDS　1998　JAPAN　SRCL4204
AD: 山崎 英樹 YAMASAKI HIDEKI　P: 浅川 英郎 ASAKAWA HIDERO　DF: STOVE INC

front

back

LUNCH FOR EAR　　*LUNCH FOR EAR*
MIDI CREATIVE　1999　JAPAN　CXCA-1045

b-flower　　*b-flower*
TOSHIBA EMI　1998　JAPAN　TOCT10223
AD, D: 坂村 健次 KENJI SAKAMURA　P: 外山 繁 SHIGERU TOYAMA
DF: コロムビア・クリエイティヴ COLUMBIA CREATIVE INC.

LITTLE SWALLOW SAKANA

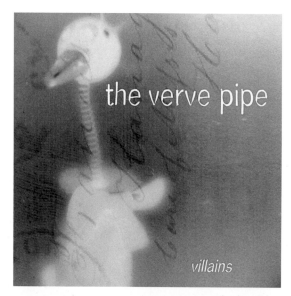

the verve pipe

villains

LITTLE SWALLOW
SAKANA

BAD NEWS 1998 JAPAN BN-110
AD, D: 角田 純一 JUNICHI TSUNODA
P: 田附 勝 MASARU TATSUKI
I: 西脇 一弘 KAZUHIRO NISHIWAKI
DF: ㈲マナス MANAS INC.

VILLAINS *THE VERVE PIPE*

RCA RECORDS 1997
USA RCA07863 66809-2
AD, D: SEAN MOSHER-SMITH
P: SLOW HEARTH STUDIO

DasDeutscheHandwerk
SINGLES '96-'99

White Trash Heroes

SINGLES '96-'99
DAS DEUTSCHE HANDWERK

DAS DEUTSCHE HANDWERK 1999 GERMANY
CD: OLIVER-A KRIMMEL, ANJA OSTERWALDER
P: I_D TEAM DF: I_D BÜRO

WHITE TRASH HEROES
ARCHERS OF LOAF

ALIAS RECORDS 1998 USA A128
CD, AD, D: COLE GERST
P: MICHAEL TRAISTER

Washingtonia Washingtonia

☆LIFETIME
&LIVING? *%
GRAPEVINE

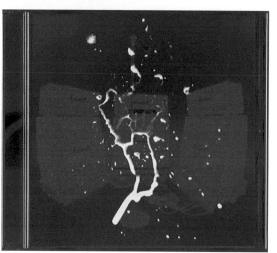

LIFETIME *GRAPEVINE*

PONY CANYON 1999 JAPAN PCCA-01332
AD: 角田 純一 JUNICHI TSUNODA
D: 田中 純子 JUNKO TANAKA
P: 塩田 正幸 MASAYUKI SHIODA
DF: ㈲マナス MANAS INC.

Useless Music *WINO*

VICTOR ENTERTAINMENT 1999 JAPAN
VICL-60348

front without case

front

inner

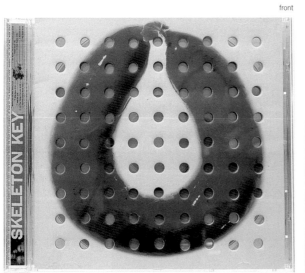

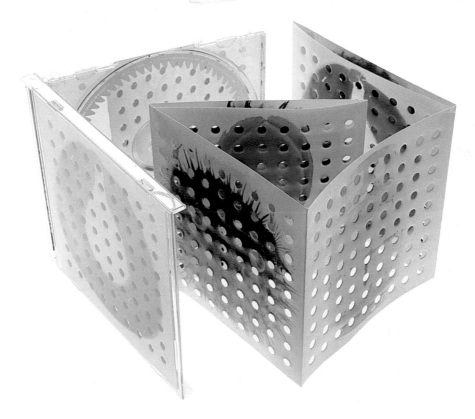

FANTASTIC SPIKES THROUGH BALLOON   *SKELETON KEY*

CAPITOL RECORDS 1997 USA CDP7243 8 36688 23
CD, AD: STEFAN SAGMEISTER D: HJALTI KARLSSON P: TOM SCHIERLITZ CW: SKELETON KEY DF: SAGMEISTER INC.

front

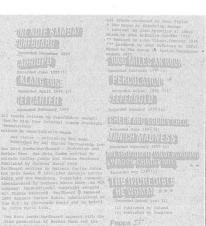

inner

ALUMINUM TUNES   *STEREOLAB*

DUOPHONIC UHF DISKS 1998 UK DC159CD

AMELIA   *LONG FIN KILLIE*
TOKUMA JAPAN COMMUNICATIONS   1997   JAPAN   TKCB71259

TRI-DANIELSON!!!（OMEGA）   *DANIELSON*
TOOTH AND NAIL RECORDS   1999   USA   TND1114
AD,D : DANIEL SMITH   LETTERING: CHRISTIAAN PALLADINO
COMPUTER PRODUCTION: MARC D'AGUSTO
MECHANICS: LENNY SMITH   DF: LOOKS FAMILYRE

SOLAR ECLIPSE   *V.A.*
GREEN RECORDS   1997   JAPAN   GREEN003
CD: 渡辺 美智代 MICHIYO WATANABE   D: 上野 光生 MITSUO UENO

ANALOG *SOLVEIG*
MEGA SCANDINAVIA 1998 DENMARK MRCD3380

STAY AWAY FROM THE WINDOWS   *CHICKENPOX*
BURNING HEART RECORDS   1998   SWEDEN   BHR074

THE JULIA FORDHAM COLLECTION   *JULIA FORDHAM*
VIRGIN RECORDS   1998   UK   CIRCD36   7243 8 46315 2 9

eden.vmg.co.uk/juliafordham

TOCP-50411

GOOD HUMOR   *SAINT ETIENNE*
TOSHIBA EMI   1998   JAPAN   TOCP50411

ANALOG   *SOLVEIG*
VICTOR ENTERTAINMENT   1999   JAPAN   VICP60563

THIS CONVERSATION IS ENDING   STARTING RIGHT NOW
KNAPSACK
ALIAS RECORDS 1998 USA A136-2
CD, AD, D, I: COLE GERST P: PETER ELLENBY

LEVI'S COLORS   *HIPSTAR IMAGE*
POLYGRAM 1999 JAPAN UDSP-32
CD: STANLEY WONG   AD, I: TONY WILLIAMS

UNIVERSAL MADNESS   *MADNESS*
GOLDENVOICE 1998 USA 44402-2

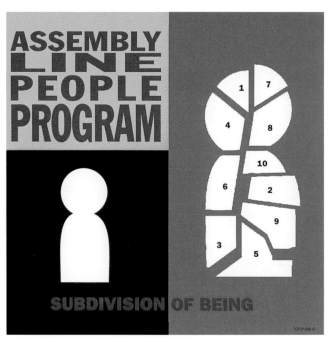

ASSEMBLY LINE PEOPLE PROGRAM   *SUBDIVISION OF BEING*
TOSHIBA EMI 1998 JAPAN TOCP50612

ハワイアン ラプソディ HAWAIIAN RHAPSODY
吉田 拓郎 TAKURO YOSHIDA
FOR LIFE 1998 JAPAN FLCF-3733
CD: 仲島 圭市 KEIICHI NAKAJIMA、渡辺 富夫 TOMIO WATANABE AD: ROCKET
D: セキ ユリヲ YURIO SEKI I: 谷本 ヨーコ YOKO TANIMOTO

case front

front

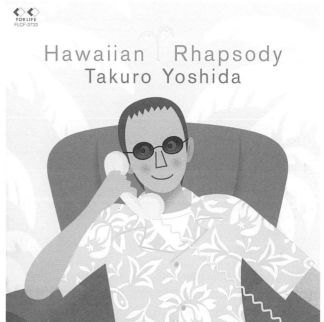

front

TOKYO THE REMIXES V.A.
BUNGALOW 1998 GERMANY BUNG053

booklet

PREGO! '99 CAMP-MASTER *V.A.*

TRATTORIA 1999 JAPAN PSCR5746   front   sleeve

disk

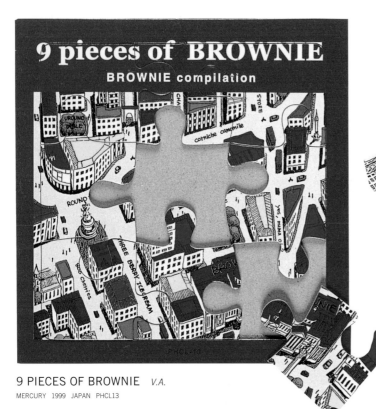

9 PIECES OF BROWNIE *V.A.*

MERCURY 1999 JAPAN PHCL13

WALKIN' ON EGGS   *NIGHTHAWKS AT THE DINER*
A-RECORDS 1998 THE NETHERLANDS AL73136

DARE TO BE SURPRISED   *THE FOLK IMPLOSION*
COMMUNION 1997 USA COMM45

今じゃない まだ早い ような   IMA JANAI MADA HAYAI YOUNA   *CYCLES*
Ki/oon RECORDS 1999 JAPAN KSC2296

case front

disk

SMAP 011 ス   SMAP 011 SU   *SMAP*

VICTOR ENTERTAINMENT 1997 JAPAN VICL60052

inner without disk

THE SPECIAL GOODNESS *PATRICK WILSON*

ROCK RECORDS (JAPAN) 1998 JAPAN RCCY-1025

DISCO SUCKS *V.A.*

CHE TRADING 1996 UK CHE60CD
D: ANDREW CLARE

PUNK BREAK OUT USA *V.A.*

FLAVOUR OF SOUND 1998 JAPAN TFCK-87587

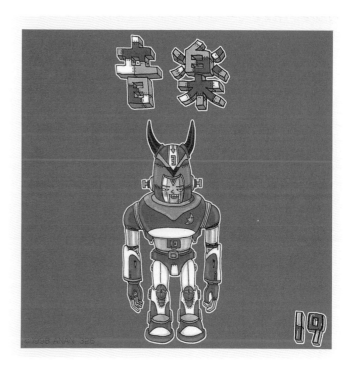

音楽 ONGAKU *19（ジューク）JUKU*

VICTOR ENTERTAINMENT 1999 JAPAN VICL-60442
AD, D, I: 326

front

back

inner

FEELINGS *DAVID BYRNE*

WARNER BROS. RECORDS 1997 USA 9 46605-2
CD, AD: STEFAN SAGMEISTER   D: HJALTI KARLSSON
P: TOM SCHIERLITZ CW: DAVID BYRNE
MODEL MAKER: YUJI YOSHIMOTO DF: SAGMEISTER INC.

NOW PLAYING *CHOPPER ONE*
BMG FUNHOUSE 1998 JAPAN BVCP6108

Soundtrack from " RUNABOUT " *THE SURF COASTERS*
VICTOR ENTERTAINMENT 1997 JAPAN VICL60028

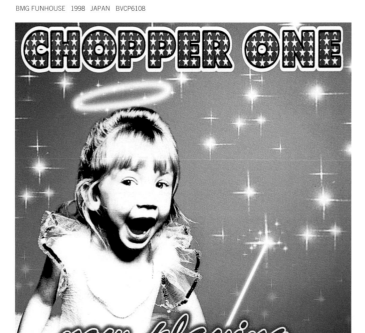

BREATHING TORNADOS *BEN LEE*
TOSHIBA EMI 1999 JAPAN TOCP-65086

GROOVIN' TIME   *IMAWANO KIYOSHIRO LITTLE SCREAMING REVUE*

TOSHIBA EMI   1997   JAPAN   TOCT-9911
AD, D: 角田 純一 JUNICHI TSUNODA   D: 田中 純子 JUNKO TANAKA   P: 大森 克己 KATSUMI OMORI
I: 五木田 智央 TOMOO GOKITA   DF: ㈲マナス MANAS INC.

PENNSYLVANIA   *PERE UBU*

COOKING VINYL   1998   UK   COOKCD139

POP AMERICAN STYLE   SPECIAL DELIVERY   *V.A.*

FLAVOUR OF SOUND   1997   JAPAN   TFCK-87573
ARTWORK, DESIGN, & LAYOUT: SHERIA SACHS & SKIPPY

THRU MY WINDOW   *JEFFREY FOSKETT*

PIONEER LDC   1996   JAPAN   PICP1115

ロメオの心臓 ROMEO'S HEART　*BLANKEY JET CITY*

POLYDOR　1998　JAPAN　POCH-1708
CD, AD: 信藤 三雄 MITSUO SHINDO　D: 大箭 亮二 RYOJI OHYA　P: 田島 一成 KAZUNARI TAJIMA
DF: コンテムポラリー・プロダクション CONTEMPORARY PRODUCTION

back　　　　　　　　　　　　　　　　　　　　　　　　　　　　　　　　　　front

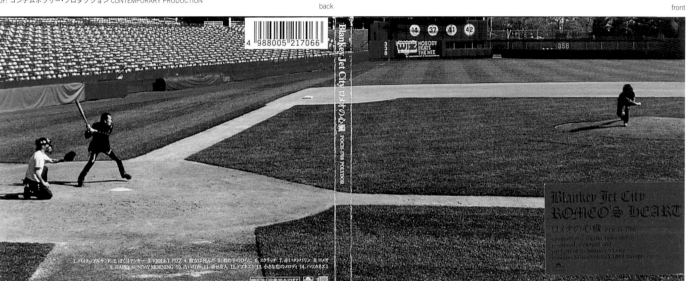

ヤングフラワーズ YOUNG FLOWERS
フラワーカンパニーズ *FLOWER COMPANYZ*

ANTINOS RECORDS　1997　JAPAN　ARCJ71

THE ALBEMARLE SOUND　*THE LADYBUG TRANSISTOR*

MERGE RECORDS　1999　USA　MRG154CD

SO FAR, SO GOOD THE MARCH RECORDS STORY (1992-1998)
V.A.

MARCH RECORDS / ROCK RECORDS (JAPAN) 1999 JAPAN RCCY1040

HAVE LEFT THE PLANET   *THE DEVIANTS*

CAPTAIN TRIP RECORDS 1999 JAPAN CTCD-163

CONTINENTAL   *SAINT ETIENNE*

NIPPON COLUMBIA 1997 JAPAN COCY80608

THE LAST GOODBYE   *SPRING*
ELEFANT RECORDS 1998 SPAIN ER1052
D: MAGIC DESIGN

GET IN   *KENICKIE*
TOSHIBA EMI 1998 JAPAN TOCP50719

SUICAINE GRATIFACTION   *PAUL WESTERBERG*
CAPITOL RECORDS   1999   USA   CDP7243 4 98939 2 4

front

inner without disk

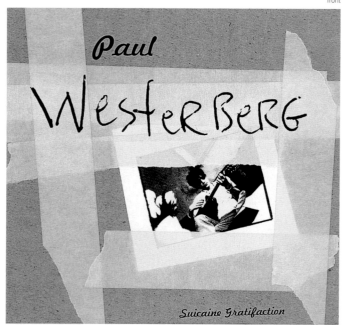

月を超えろ TSUKI WO KOERO   奥田 民生 *OKUDA TAMIO*
SME RECORDS   1999   JAPAN   SRCL4507
AD: 山崎 英樹 YAMASAKI HIDEKI   P: 三浦 憲治 MIURA KENJI   DF: STOVE INC

NEVER HOME   *FREEDY JOHNSTON*
ELEKTRA   1997   USA   61920-2

Album artwork used courtesy of
Elektra Entertainment Group Inc.

PANIC BOOM *PONOI*

MIDI CREATIVE 1999 JAPAN CXCA-1044

BELIEVE *MISIA*

BMG FUNHOUSE 1999 JAPAN BVCS-29008
AD: 信藤 三雄 MITSUO SHINDO D: 新家 敏之 TOSHIYUKI SHINKE P: 富永 よしえ YOSHIE TOMINAGA
DF: コンテムポラリー・プロダクション CONTEMPORARY PRODUCTION

back

front

MIND *EINS·VIER*

MELDAC 1997 JAPAN MECR30106
AD, D, DF: ㈲サイレントグラフィックス SILENT GRAPHICS, INC. P: 長峯 正幸 MASAYUKI NAGAMINE

front

OUT SPACED *SUPER FURRY ANIMALS*
CREATION RECORDS 1998 UK CRECD229L
DF: INFLATE LTD

booklet

RECUBED EP *TAKAKO MINEKAWA*
POLYSTAR 1999 JAPAN PSCR-5730
D: TAKAKO MINEKAWA, 土肥 雅樹 MASAKI DOHI

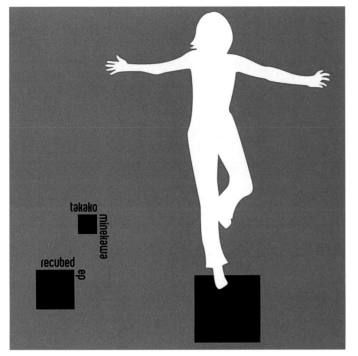

XIMER *TAKAKO MINEKAWA*
EMPEROR NORTON RECORDS 1999 USA EMN7019-2
AD: COLE GERST D: COLE GERST / GEMINI

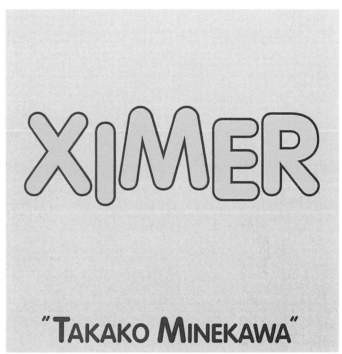

YOYO A GOGO *V.A.*
YOYO RECORDINGS 1998 USA YOYOCD-10
D: PAT CASTALDO

THE BEST Love Winters 広瀬 香美 *HIROSE KOHMI*
VICTOR ENTERTAINMENT 1998 JAPAN VICL-60305

コドモ Z　KODOMO Z　*CASCADE*
VICTOR ENTERTAINMENT　1999　JAPAN　VICL-60354

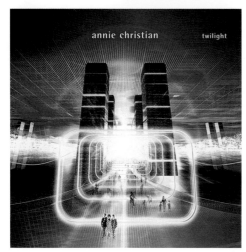

TWILIGHT　*ANNIE CHRISTIAN*

V2 MUSIC　1999　UK　V2CI31
DESIGN / ILLUSTRATION BY MR. MURDOCH@SATELLITE

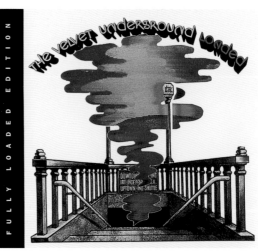

LOADED FULLY LOADED EDITION
THE VELVET UNDERGROUND

EAST WEST JAPAN　1997　JAPAN　AMCY-2087~8

RUSHES *THE FIREMAN*
TOSHIBA EMI 1998 JAPAN TOCP65018

A LAKE OF TEARDROPS
SPECTRUM & SILVER APPLES

SPACE AGE RECORDINGS 1998 UK ORBIT016CD

VERSION2.0 *GARBAGE*
BMG FUNHOUSE 1998 JAPAN BVCP6119

MIGHTY BLOW *THE COLLECTORS*

fold-out sleeve

NIPPON COLUMBIA 1996 JAPAN COCA13616
AD: 駿東 宏 HIROSHI SUNTO AD, D: 加藤 靖隆 YASUTAKA KATO P: 三浦 憲治 KENJI MIURA

BUSTER'S SPANISH ROCKET SHIP *BUSTER POINDEXTER*

ISLAND RECORDS 1997 USA 314-524 414-2
AD, D: SPENCER DRATE AD: JÜTKA SALAVETZ D: DENNIS ASCIENZO
P: DAVID LACHAPELLE STUDIO DF: SPENCER DRATE, JUSTDESIGN

DISTORTION LOVE *KENJI SAWADA*

TOSHIBA EMI 1997 JAPAN TOCT-10018
AD: TAKEJI HAYAKAWA D: KAZU ABE (RHYTHMIC GARDEN)
P: ARAO YOKOGI COSTUME DESIGN: TAKEJI HAYAKAWA

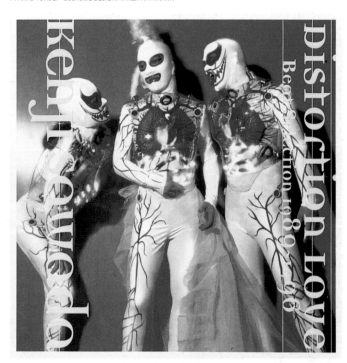

ELECTRO ASYL-BOP *SOUL FLOWER UNION*

Ki/oon RECORDS 1996 JAPAN KSC2164
AD, D: 加藤 靖隆 YASUTAKA KATO P: 内貴 太郎 TARO NAIKI

ABYSS TO ABYSS *UNDERCURRENT*

MIDI CREATIVE 1999 JAPAN CXCA-1053
AD, D: 加藤 靖隆 YASUTAKA KATO P: 大野 純一 JUNICHI ONO I: 杖村 さえ子 SAEKO TSUEMURA

DOUBLE DATE WITH JOANIE AND CHACHI   *V.A.*

NICK AT NITE RECORD 1997 USA BK63456
CD: KENNA KAY, NICK ELODEON   D, I: MELINDA BECK   DF: MELINDA BECK STUDIO

LET'S TALK ABOUT FEELINGS   *LAGWAGON*

FAT WRECK CHORDS 1998 USA FAT578-2

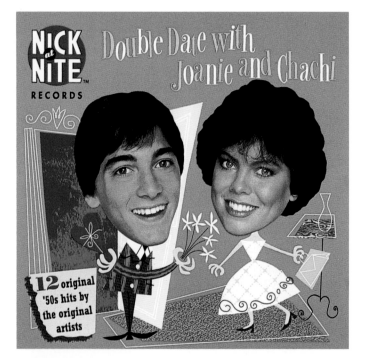

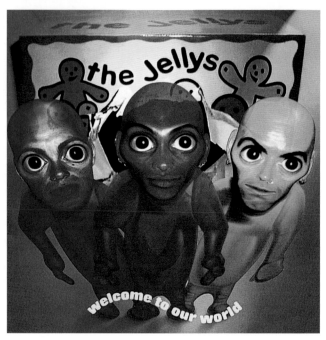

WELCOME TO OUR WORLD   *THE JELLYS*

avex trax 1999 JAPAN AVCM

CHILDREN CAN BE SO CRUEL   *GOD IS MY CO-PILOT*

MIGUEL 1998 USA 1
CD, D, I: MELINDA BECK   DF: MELINDA BECK STUDIO

SOL *LOST CANDI*

Ki/oon RECORDS 1997 JAPAN KSC2192
D: 坂村 健次 KENJI SAKAMURA P: 三宅 勝士 SHOJI MIYAKE DF: コロムビア・クリエイティヴ COLUMBIA CREATIVE INC.

KEEP IT LIKE A SECRET *BUILT TO SPILL*

WARNER BROS. RECORDS 1999 USA 9 46952-2

中古の円盤 CHUKO NO ENBAN *SUPER TRAPP*

BMG FUNHOUSE 1998 JAPAN BVCS-29003（74321-61579-2)
AD, D, DF: ㈲サイレントグラフィックス SILENT GRAPHICS, INC.

ズックにロック ZUKKU NI ROCK
ゆらゆら帝国 *YURAYURA TEIKOKU*

MIDI 1999 JAPAN MDCS1022

HELLOFATESTER *RASMUS*
WARNER MUSIC FINLAND 1998 FINLAND 3984-25728-2

front

disk

LOLLO ROSSO *THE HIGH LLAMAS*
V2 MUSIC 1998 UK VVR1002582
ART DIRECTION: M2 AND SEAN O'HAGAN DESIGN BY M2

SECONDS *SEELY*
TOKUMA JAPAN COMMUNICATIONS 1997 JAPAN TKCB71243

DOTSANDLOOPS *STEREOLAB*
DUOPHONIC UHF DISKS 1997 UK 7559-62065-2

BUTTERFLIES *JZ BARRELL AND BUTTERFLIES*

Ng RECORDS 1997 USA 70618-20012-2

PUT THE NEEDLE ON THE RECORD *V.A.*

TOSHIBA EMI 1999 JAPAN TOCP65094

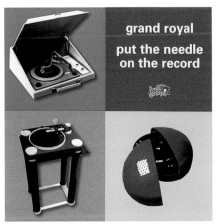

FLOË ËSSI AND ËKTAH *MAGMA*

SEVENTH RECORDS 1998 FRANCE HMCD29

UNSAFE *ALAN JONES SEXTET*

SELF RELEASED 1998 USA
AD: JOSHUA BERGER, NIKO COURTELIS, PETE McCRACKEN
D: DYLAN NELSON DF: PLAZM DESIGN

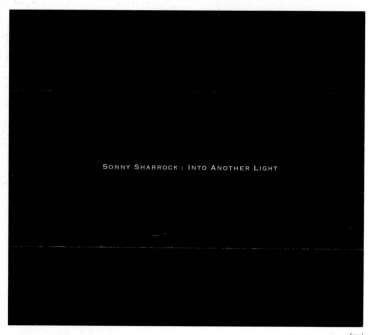

front

disk

INTO ANOTHER LIGHT *SONNY SHARROCK*

ENEMY RECORDS 1997 USA EMY156-2
CD, AD: STEFAN SAGMEISTER D: VERONICA OH P: ADAM FUSS DF: SAGMEISTER INC.

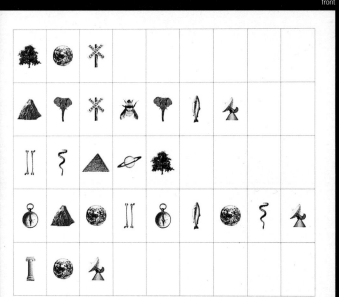

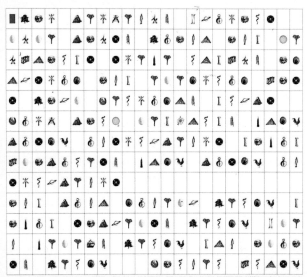

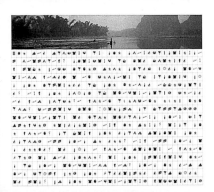

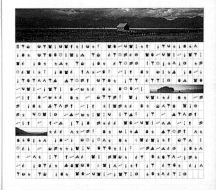

IMAGINARY DAY   *PAT METHENY GROUP*

WARNER BROS. RECORDS 1997 USA WARNER BROS. 2-46821
CD, AD: STEFAN SAGMEISTER   D: HJALTI KARLSSON
P: TOM SCHIERLITZ, STOCK   CW: PAT METHENY   DF: SAGMEISTER INC.

front

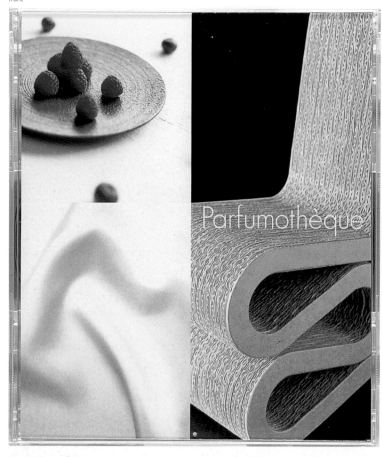

back

PARFUMOTHÈQUE *PARFUMOTHÈQUE*

BANDAI MUSIC 1999 JAPAN APCA-267
D: 小林 孝至 KOBAYASHI TAXI

front

back

NATURAL LIFE WITH IDÉE *V.A.*

WARNER MUSIC JAPAN 1999 JAPAN
WPCR-10311
D: TATS OHISA FOR MODERN MODE

natural life with **IDÉE** flowers, furniture and sounds in your space.

01	I Want You Back	The Esso Trinidad Steel Band
02	For What It's Worth	Buffalo Springfield
03	Only So Much Oil In The Ground	Tower Of Power
04	Long Train Runnin'	The Doobie Brothers
05	Venga Venga	Jo Mama
06	Wiggle Waggle	Herbie Hancock
07	Temptation	Eric Justin Kaz
08	Still Feeling Blue	Gram Parsons
09	Talkin' About Jesus	Delaney & Bonnie & Friends
10	Spanish Moon	Little Feat
11	What Is This?	Sergio Mendes
12	Morning Worship	Alice Coltrane
13	Come Together	Sara Vaughan

front

back

pop life with **IDÉE** flowers, furniture and sounds in your space.

01	Spring Song	Linda Lewis
02	One Way Or The Other	The Fifth Avenue Band
03	Sugar Sugar Honey	Cultured Pearls
04	Diagonals	Stereolab
05	One Note Samba	Antonio Carlos Jobim
06	Half A Minute	Elektrostar
07	Steelband Music	Van Dyke Parks
08	Un Woman's Paradis	Dimitri From Paris
09	The Night We Flew Out The Window	Fantastic Something
10	59th Street Bridge Song (Feelin' Groovy)	Harpers Bizarre
11	Someday Man	Paul Williams
12	Sugarbird	Jimmy Webb
13	Let's Go To Brazil	The Hi-Lo's
14	Tin Tin Por Tin Tin	Joao Gilberto
15	Something	Sarah Vaughan
16	Like A Seed	Kenny Rankin

POP LIFE WITH IDÉE *V.A.*

WARNER MUSIC JAPAN 1999 JAPAN
WPCR-10312
D: TATS OHISA FOR MODERN MODE

front

back

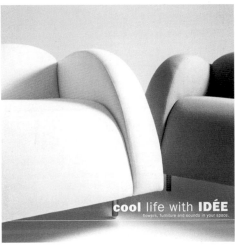

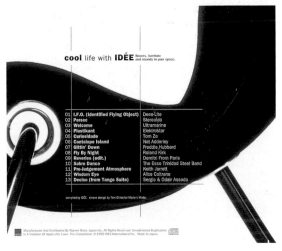

cool life with **IDÉE** flowers, furniture and sounds in your space.

01	I.F.O. (Identified Flying Object)	Deee-Lite
02	Parsec	Stereolab
03	Welcome	Ultramarine
04	Plastikant	Elektrostar
05	Curlosidade	Tom Zé
06	Cantaloupe Island	Nat Adderley
07	Gittin' Down	Freddie Hubbard
08	Fly By Night	Roland Kirk
09	Reveries (edit.)	Demitri From Paris
10	Sabre Dance	The Esso Trinidad Steel Band
11	Pre-Judgement Atmosphere	Keith Jarrett
12	Wisdom Eye	Alice Coltrane
13	Deciso (from Tango Suite)	Sergio & Odair Assado

COOL LIFE WITH IDÉE *V.A.*

WARNER MUSIC JAPAN 1999 JAPAN
WPCR-10310
D: TATS OHISA FOR MODERN MODE

ECLIPSE DE LUNA *RAFAEL CORTEZ*
ETHNO ART 1998 GERMANY 20018
CD, AD, D: JOERG WASCHAT   P: PHILIP LETHEN   DF: VS.42 DESIGNSTUDIO

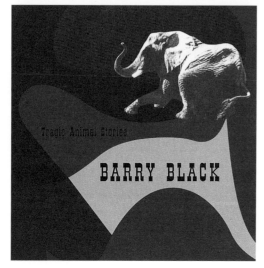

TRAGIC ANIMAL STORIES *BARRY BLACK*

ALIAS RECORDS 1997 USA A122
CD, AD, D: COLE GERST

SOMOS ADÚ *FÉLIX CASAVERDE*

BOMBA RECORDS 1999 JAPAN BOM22093
D: 根岸 秀行 HIDEYUKI NEGISHI

CANTARE, MANGIARE #PRIMO *V.A.*
EAST WEST JAPAN 1999 JAPAN AMCE-7009

A PRENDRE *MIOSSEC*
ALTER-POP 1998 JAPAN ERPCD-5920

BEST OF ENZO ENZO *ENZO ENZO*
BMG FUNHOUSE 1998 JAPAN BVCP21004

FOREVER & EVER *DUNE & THE LONDON SESSION ORCHESTRA*

ORBIT RECORDS 1998 GERMANY 8 46965 2
AD, D, I: EIKE KOENIG & RALF HIEMISCH DF: EIKES GRAFISCHER HORT

GUN HAZARD ORIGINAL SOUNDTRACK

NTT PUBLISHING 1996 JAPAN PSCN-5044~5
CD, AD, D: 島田 忠司 TADASHI SHIMADA D: 門倉 徳映 NORIE KADOKURA
P: 広瀬 忠司 TADASHI HIROSE DF: ㈲バナナスタジオ BANANA STUDIO INC.

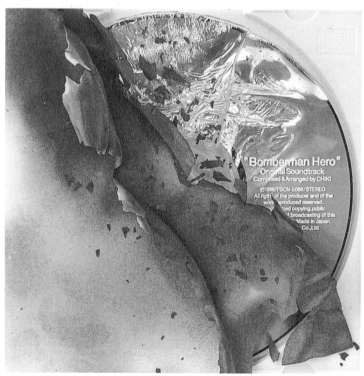

BOMBERMAN HERO ORIGINAL SOUNDTRACK

NTT PUBLISHING 1998 JAPAN PSCN-5066
CD, AD, D: 島田 忠司 TADASHI SHIMADA D: 門倉 徳映 NORIE KADOKURA
P: 柴泉 寛 HIROSHI SHIBAIZUMI, 大竹 肖治 SHOJI OTAKE DF: ㈲バナナスタジオ BANANA STUDIO INC.

SMAPPIES II *V.A.*

VICTOR ENTERTAINMENT 1999 JAPAN VICP60719
AD: 信藤 三雄 MITSUO SHINDO D: 北澤 剛志 TAKESHI KITAZAWA
DF: コンテムポラリー・プロダクション CONTEMPORARY PRODUCTION

FOREVER *DUNE AND THE LONDON SESSION ORCHESTRA*
ORBIT RECORDS 1997 GERMANY PROMO CD/LIMITED EDITION
AD, D, I: EIKE KOENIG & RALF HIEMISCH DF: EIKES GRAFISCHER HORT

front

back

inner left

inner right

CHANSONS FRANCAISES *NOTRE-DAME*

QUINCE RECORDS 1998 JAPAN QRCP-9008
D: ARNAUD FLEURENT-DIDIER

front

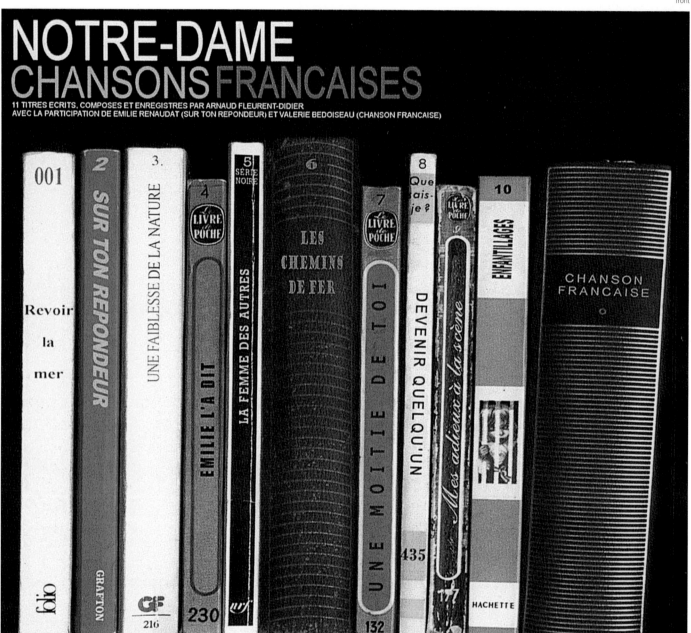

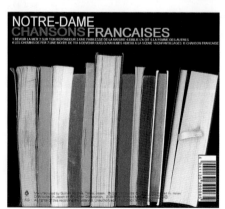

back

MUSIC OF FADING CULTURES（PIECES OF TIME）
ONE LITTLE CREATURE

VIRGIN RECORDS 1998 UK VJCP-68011

TELLING STORIES TO THE SEA *V.A.*

LUAKA BOP 1997 USA 9 45669-2
CD, AD: STEFAN SAGMEISTER D: VERONICA OH P: TOM SCHIERLITZ
I: INDIGO ARTS CW: VARIOUS DF: SAGMEISTER INC.

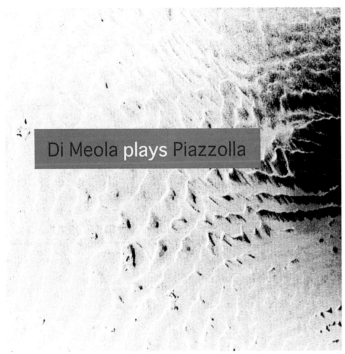

DI MEOLA PLAYS PIAZZOLLA *AL DI MEOLA*

FLAVOUR OF SOUND 1997 JAPAN TFCK-87550
AD, D, P: RICHARD EVANS

PERPETUAL WORKS BEST OF AL DI MEOLA *AL DI MEOLA*

FLAVOUR OF SOUND 1997 JAPAN TFCK-87553

SILENCIO=MUERTE: RED HOT+LATIN   *V.A.*

THE RED HOT ORGANIZATION   1996   USA   119 341 005 2

front

jewel case

front

jewel case

REDHOT+RIO   *V.A.*

THE RED HOT ORGANIZATION   1996   USA   533 183-2

booklet

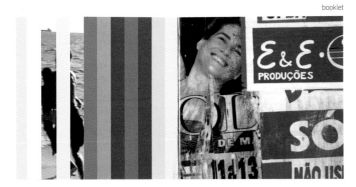

front

jewel case

ONDA SONORA: RED HOT+LISBON *V.A.*

THE RED HOT ORGANIZATION 1998 USA MOV30.375

front

STAR RISE
NUSRAT FATEH ALI KHAN & MICHAEL BROOK: REMIXED

REAL WORLD RECORDS 1997 UK CDRW68
D: TRISTAN MANCO FOR REAL WORLD DESIGN

jewel case with disk

NIGHT SONG   *NUSRAT FATEH ALI KHAN & MICHAEL BROOK*

REAL WORLD RECORDS 1995 UK CDRW50
P: ROBERT LESLIE

© REAL WORLD RECORDS LTD   front

jewel case with disk

LA CANDELA VIVA   *TOTÓ LA MOMPOSINA Y SUS TAMBORES*

REAL WORLD RECORDS 1998 UK CDRW31
P: ANDREW CATLIN

© REAL WORLD RECORDS LTD

HUSSEIN MAHMOOD JEEB TEHAR GASS *MUSLIMGAUZE*

SOLEILMOON RECORDINGS 1998 USA SOL73CD
AD: JOSHUA BERGER, NIKO COURTELIS, PETE McCRACKEN AD, D: RIQ MOSQUEDA
P: SHIRIN NESHAT DF: PLAZM DESIGN

INDONESIAN SOUNDSCAPES

SOLEILMOON RECORDINGS 1999 USA SOL82CD
D, P: RIQ MOSQUEDA DF: PLAZM DESIGN

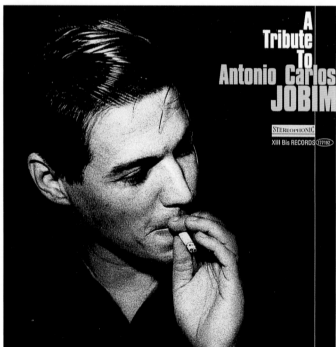

A TRIBUTE TO ANTONIO CARLOS JOBIM *V.A.*

XIII BIS RECORDS 1997 FRANCE 177192

LA PISTE AUX ÉTOILES *V.A.*

EUROPOP 2000 1998 FRANCE RÉF.178802
D: OLIVIER GODOT

inner

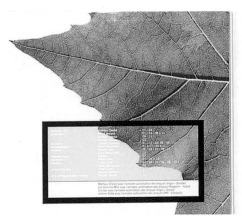  

front

back

À LA LÉGÈRE *JANE BIRKIN*

MERCURY FRANCE 1998 FRANCE 538 045-2
P: LAURENT SEROUSSI

BLUE LAGOON   *PETTY BOOKA*
NIPPON CROWN (SISTER RECORDS) 1998 JAPAN CRCS-1004
D: ROCKIN JELLY BEAN

DANCING WITH PETTY BOOKA   *PETTY BOOKA*
NIPPON CROWN (SISTER RECORDS) 1999 JAPAN CRCS-1006
D: ROCKIN JELLY BEAN

SANDII WITH THE COCONUT CUPS   *SANDII*
HORIPRO 1999 JAPAN XYCA-00040
D, I: 菊地 佐智子 SACHIKO KIKUCHI
DF: カプアラニ・グラフィックス・トーキョー KAPUALANI GRAPHICS TOKYO

SANDII'S HAWAI'I 3RD   *SANDII*
EAST WEST JAPAN 1998 JAPAN AMCY-2755
D: 菊地 佐智子 SACHIKO KIKUCHI P: 平間 至 ITARU HIRAMA
DF: カプアラニ・グラフィックス・トーキョー KAPUALANI GRAPHICS TOKYO

MARIMBA TROPICANA   *MARIMBA TROPICANA*
RESPECT RECORD 1999 JAPAN RES-27
AD, I: 笹尾 俊一 TOSHIKAZU SASAO P: 戸澤 裕司 HIROSHI TOZAWA

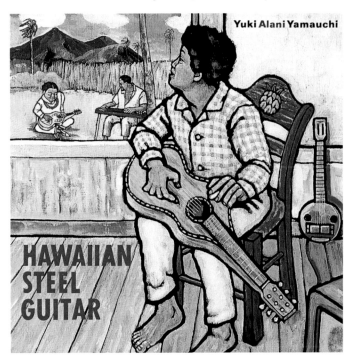

HAWAIIAN STEEL GUITAR   *YUKI ALANI YAMAUCHI*
RESPECT RECORD 1998 JAPAN RES-23
AD, I: 笹尾 俊一 TOSHIKAZU SASAO P: 垂見 健吾 KENGO TAKUMI

O DIA EM QUE FAREMOS CONTATO *LENINE*

BMG FUNHOUSE 1997 JAPAN BVCP6075

front

O SAMBA POCONÉ *SKANK*

EPIC RECORDS 1997 JAPAN ESCA6697

front

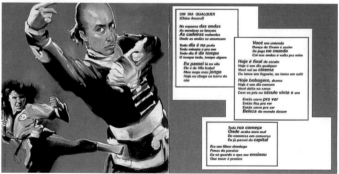

booklet

booklet

front   disk

都はるみステージカラオケコレクション
HARUMI MIYAKO
STAGE KARAOKE COLLECTION
都はるみ *HARUMI MIYAKO*

COLUMBIA 1996 JAPAN COCK-13068
CD, AD: 水谷 孝次 KOJI MIZUTANI D: 大溝 裕 HIROSHI OMIZO
I: 河村 要助 YOUSUKE KAWAMURA DF: ㈲水谷事務所 MIZUTANI STUDIO

冠 REVOLUTION　KANMURI REVOLUTION
冠 二郎 *JIRO KANMURI*

COLUMBIA 1998 JAPAN COCA50008
D: 橋本 真志 MASASHI HASHIMOTO I: 土屋 ヒデル HIDERU TSUCHIYA
DF: コロムビア・クリエイティヴ COLUMBIA CREATIVE INC.

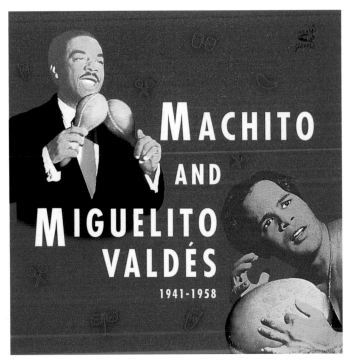

BRASIL SÃO OUTROS 500   *V.A.*

SOM LIVRE 1998 BRAZIL 5101-2
D: DANIEL DE SOUZA

MACHITO AND MIGUELITO VALDÉS 1941-1958
MACHITO AND MIGUELITO VALDÉS

UNIVERSAL VICTOR 1998 JAPAN MVCE24123

front

booklet

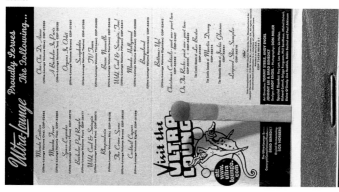

inner

ULTRA-LOUNGE *V.A.*

CAPITOL RECORDS 1999 USA CDP72434 99144 21

FUN, FUN, FUN *V.A.*

ATMOSPHERE MUSIC 1997 UK ATMOSCD87
CD, AD, D, I: RIAN HUGHES   DF: DEVICE

CLEVER KIDS *V.A.*

ATMOSPHERE MUSIC 1997 UK ATMOSCD69
CD, AD, D, I: RIAN HUGHES   DF: DEVICE

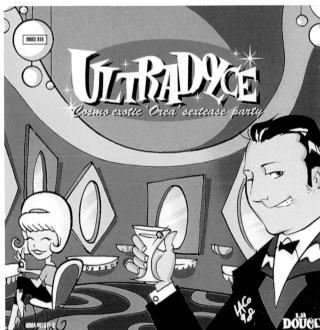

ULTRADOLCE *V.A.*

IRMA RECORDS 1998 ITALY IRMA491571-2
CD: UMBI DAMIANI   AD: ELENA FIUMI   I: JACOPO CAMAGNI

B-MOVIE HEROES *SAM PAGLIA*

IRMA RECORDS 1998 ITALY IRMA492978-2
CD: UMBI DAMIANI   AD: ELENA FIUMI   I: SAM PAGLIA

LA COLECCIÓN DE LAS CLUDADES-MÓDULO 2 *CASABLANCA*
ELEFANT RECORDS 1999 SPAIN ER-1056
D: ELEFANT DESIGN

SUPERMARKET *V.A.*
ELEFANT RECORDS 1998 SPAIN ER-1051
D: ELEFANT DESIGN

SUONO LIBERO VOLUME 2 *V.A.*
IRMA RECORDS 1998 ITALY TRMA491673-2
CD: UMBI DAMIANI AD: ELENA FIUMI I, DF: SANDRO SYMEONI

SOUND BOOK *V.A.*
IRMA RECORDS 1998 ITALY IRMA491672-2
CD: UMBI DAMIANI AD: ELENA FIUMI I, DF: SANDRO SYMEONI

front

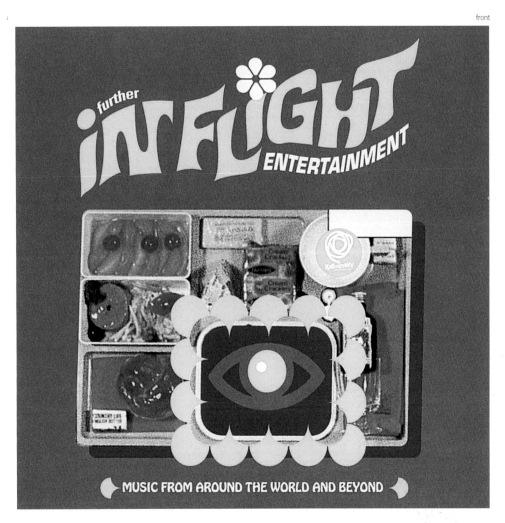

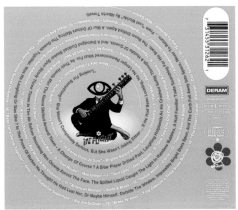

back

inner

IN FLIGHT *V.A.*

THE DECCA RECORD COMPANY 1997 UK DERAM553 126-2
CONCEIVED AND COMPILED BY THE KARMINSKY EXPERIENCE INC.

CHANTE *VALÉRIE LEMERCIER*

NIPPON COLUMBIA 1996 JAPAN COCY80393

TROPIC OF HOKUM *THE MOLESTICS*

BLUE LIZARD RECORDINGS 1997 CANADA BLR002
CD: TROY BAILLY AD: STEPHEN PARKES DF: PROTOTYPE DESIGN

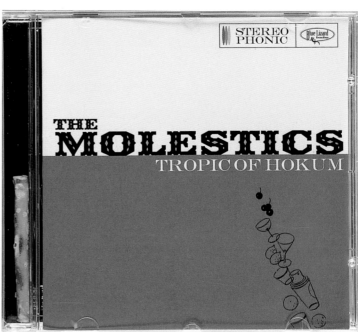

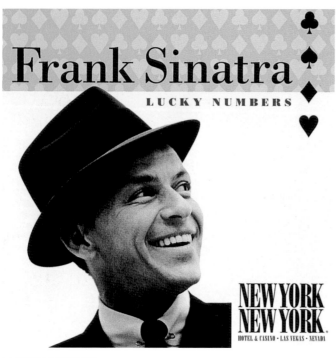

LUCKY NUMBERS *FRANK SINATRA*

REPRISE RECORDS 1998 USA 9 46853-2

DREAMS, PLEAS & BLUES *THE RAVENS*

COLUMBIA / LEGACY 1998 USA CK65260
CD: HOWARD FRITZSON AD: TIM MORSE P: MICHAEL OCHS ARCHIVES / VENICE, CA DF: COLOURED HARD INC.

ESTRATOSFERA *GASCA*
ELEFANT RECORDS 1999 SPAIN ER-319
D: ELEFANT DESIGN

front

back

stereo
⊕
ER-319

gasca

estratosfera .01
mal ladrón .02
nube gris .03
en ningún tren .04
.05

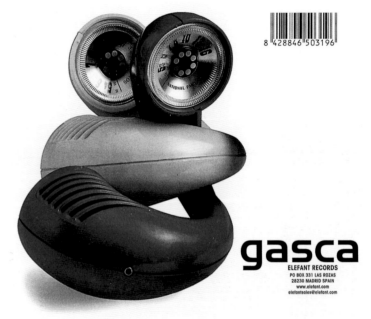

8 428846 503196

gasca
ELEFANT RECORDS
PO BOX 331 LAS ROZAS
28230 MADRID SPAIN
www.elefant.com
elefantsales@elefant.com

MORNING BEAR *EDEN*
EMI BELGIUM 1998 BELGIUM 7243 4958742 7
CD, AD, D, I: SVEN MASTBOOMS I: JEROEN VAN OMME DF: SEVEN PRODUCTIONS

MORCEAUX CHOISIS *THE RECYCLERS*
UPLINK RECORDS 1998 JAPAN ULR-003
D: JEAN LE COINTRE

1 9 9

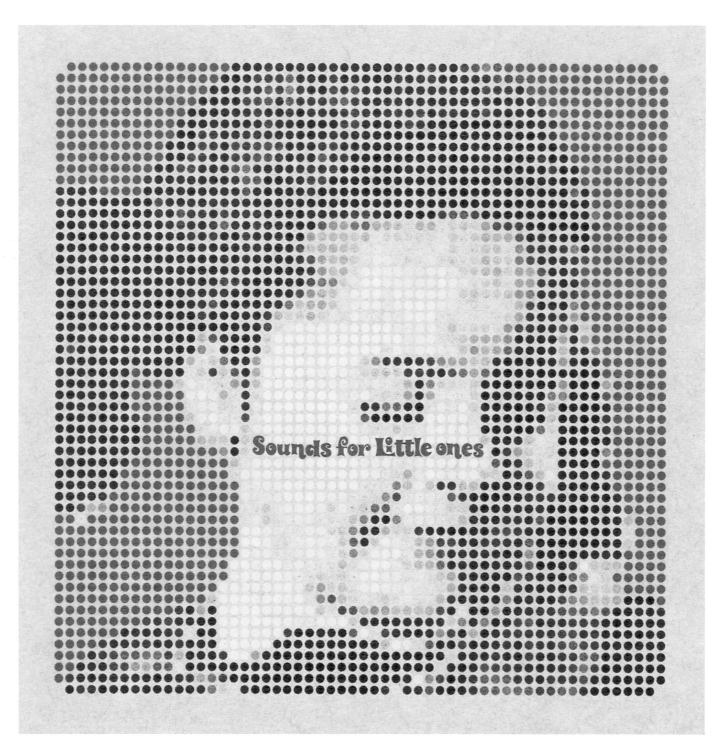

Sounds for Little ones

SOUNDS FOR LITTLE ONES   *DISH RECORDINGS*
UPLINK RECORDS 1999 JAPAN ULR-006
D: COMMAND Z（早瀬 健太郎 KENTARO HAYASE）

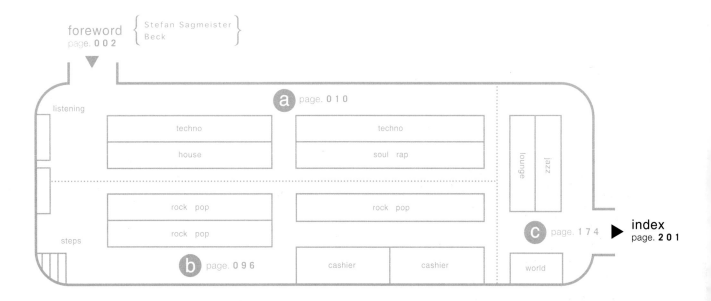

JAPAN

OVERSEAS

SUBMITTOR

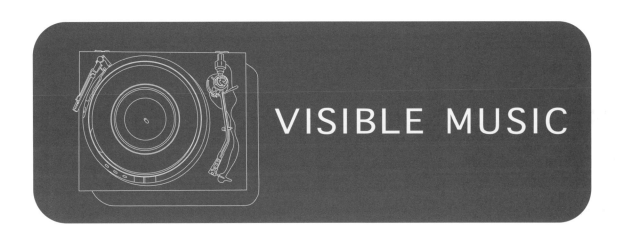

VISIBLE MUSIC

a techno
house
soul
rap

b rock
pop

c world
jazz
lounge

CD JACKET GRAPHICS

Designer:
Yutaka Ichimura

Editor:
Rika Kuwahara
Maya Kishida

Photographer:
Kuniharu Fujimoto

Translator:
Douglas Allsopp
Setsuko Noguchi

Typesetter:
Yutaka Hasegawa

Publisher:
Shingo Miyoshi

VISIBLE MUSIC
CD JACKET GRAPHICS

2000年6月20日　初版第1刷発行
定価　本体3,700円＋税

発行所　ピエ・ブックス
〒170-0003 東京都豊島区駒込4-14-6＃301
編集　Tel: 03-3949-5010 Fax: 03-3949-5650
e-mail: editor@piebooks.com
営業　Tel: 03-3940-8302 Fax: 03-3576-7361
e-mail: sales@piebooks.com

印刷・製本　（株）サンニチ印刷

©2000 by P·I·E BOOKS

ISBN 4-89444-084-9 C3070

Printed in Japan

本書の収録内容の無断転載複写、引用等を禁じます。
落丁、乱丁はお取り替えいたします。

VISIBLE MUSIC

Leo Burnett

Date Due	
27/3/01 SEONG	
5/12/01 OonSoon	
3/9/02 Javali	
17/9/02 Sfong	
20/1/03 Ahmad	
9/7/03 Yuyao	

THIS ITEM MUST BE RETURNED TO LIBRARY
BERORE THE LAST DATE ENTERED ABOVE.

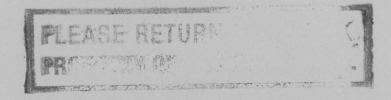